Rapture Wars
The Great End Time Debate Over Rapture

Introduction pg. 2

Chapter 1: Why Is Rapture Important pg. 8
Chapter 2: What Is Rapture pg. 32
Chapter 3: Why Is There a Debate Over Rapture pg. 37
Chapter 4: Darby and Dispensationalism pg. 46
Chapter 5: Literal or Allegorical Interpretation pg. 62
Chapter 6: Does Jesus Teach on Rapture pg. 77
Chapter 7: The Sign of Christs Presence pg. 85
Chapter 8: First Fruits and Harvest pg. 96
Chapter 9: The Rapture During Tribulation pg. 115
Chapter 10: Multiple Rapture Teachers pg. 124
Chapter 11: The Rapture Escape into Safety pg. 144
Chapter 12: What Is the Great Apostasy pg.159
Chapter 13: Christians Victory Over Antichrist pg. 167
Chapter 14: Objections to Multiple Raptures pg.178

Conclusion: Why End time Rapture Wars pg. 190

Introduction
Looking for the Blessed Hope

The unannounced hour of our Lord's return makes imperative constant readiness. As a prophet foretelling His own Advent, our Lord gives to His disciples' emphatic and pointed warnings to watchful readiness (Matt. 24. and 25.).

"WATCH ... lest coming suddenly He find YOU sleeping. And what I say unto YOU, I say unto all, WATCH" (Mark 13: 36-37). Speaking as one with authority, our Lord begins and ends this solemn Advent-warning with the single, explicit command to WATCH!

Christians who are really preparing for the Lord's impending Advent are to-day living in the ever-vigilant attitude of heart, life and conduct that springs from one constant and predominating aim - that they may be accounted worthy to escape the Judgment Wrath that is now coming swiftly upon the end of this Age.

Luke 21: 34-36 makes it startling and plain that translation is an escape from judgment. Many are taking for granted that they are ready to escape. How presumptuous their assumption when contrasted to the example Scripture sets before us in Paul! In anticipation he writes to the Philippians:-"Not that I have already attained, either were already perfect: but I follow after ... I Press towards the mark for the Prize."

Paul lived out his daily Christian experience as a man running a race with the purpose in view of winning the prize. He stripped himself in his race for the crown laid up for all of them who overcome and live godly in Christ Jesus (Rev. 12: 11). Thus, Paul could say "Thanks be unto God who always causeth us to triumph in Christ." That he might be a victor and not a victim of his circumstances Paul put heart and soul into his Christian experience. He strained every nerve, bent every muscle to apprehend that for which Christ apprehended him. Not long before Paul departed, he evidently attained to the high calling of God in Christ, for he said, "I am ready now ... I have fought a good fight, I have finished the course, I have kept the faith ... henceforth there is laid up for me a crown ... which the Lord ... shall give me in that day." What a rapturous assurance was Paul's! And it may be ours, if we, like Paul, press into the overcoming that make us more than conquerors over the world, the flesh and Satan.

Enoch was translated because he had the testimony that he pleased God. The carnal mind is enmity against God. Can we, therefore, hope to walk with God and please Him if we have any carnality, fleshliness, earthliness in us? "I, brethren, could not speak unto you as unto spiritual, but as unto carnal ... for ye are yet carnal: for whereas there is among you envying and strife, and divisions, are ye not carnal and walk as men?" (1 Cor. 3).

The words "WATCH" and "PRAY" are constantly on the lips of our Lord when warning of His sudden thief-like returning. All teaching, all preaching, all activity which annuls the Lord's solemn warning to His own to take heed to themselves and watch and pray always makes for dangerous alertness. This is the reason why many Christians to-day are walking carelessly, as though going to a picnic, when as a matter of fact, we are in the very hour of the Advent and judgment has already begun at His Sanctuary. The rapture itself is a token of that judgment on those who are left. Hence the whole strategy of Satan is to prevent the vigilance and alertness the Lord has so solemnly counselled.

"So, shall also the coming of the Son of man be. There shall two be in a field: one shall be taken and the other left ... WATCH, therefore, for ye know not what hour your Lord doth come" (Matt. 24: 39-42).

It has been said the only difference between the one the Lord takes in translation and the one left to earth's last judgments is the difference of watchful readiness. In His last discourses our Lord sought to rouse with exhortations to watchfulness the unwatchful disciple, the "robbed goodman of the house," and the unfaithful steward (Matt. 24 and 25).

"Watch therefore for ye know neither the day nor the hour when the Son of Man cometh." Christ made ever pressing the necessity of being ever ready. "Let your loins be girded about, and your lights burning: and ye yourselves like unto men that wait for their Lord ... Blessed are those servants, whom the Lord when He cometh shall find WATCHING" (Luke 12: 35-37).

We stand on the threshold of Christ's returning. Every tick of the clock draws us nearer. The darkness of earth's midnight is overspreading. The coming of the Bridegroom is at hand. Hence His Bride is making herself ready. The Spirit of the Antichrist is abroad in the world. The great tribulation is casting its shadows before. Christians, look up! Be instantly ready, vigilant, watchful; "Now is the time for you to wake out of sleep; for now, is salvation nearer to us than when we first believed. The night is far spent, and the day is at hand" (Rom. 13: 11, 12).

An almost imperceptible spiritual movement is at work in the hearts of all true believers separating the gold from the dross, the real from the unreal, the precious from the vile, the chaff from the wheat. It comes like a sacred hush upon the soul, the overshadowing of the Presence drawing near.

Christ is coming! Be ready when He comes. Separate yourself from the world's indulgence. Disentangle yourself from your immersion in the affairs of this life. Watch and pray always! A carnal Christian cannot be watchful. We can only watch as we keep spiritually awake. The word "Watch" means to be spiritually aroused, to be on the constant alert. "I sleep, but my heart waketh; it is the voice of my beloved that knocketh, saying, Open to me ... my dove, my undefiled, for my head is filled with dew, and my locks with the drops of the night" (S. of S. 5: 2).

He is coming when we think not. There is to be no warning. "As the lightning cometh out of the east, and shineth even unto the west, so shall also the coming of the Son of Man be" (Matt. 24: 27). One quick, blinding flash and the watchful will be with the Lord. The unwatchful according to our Lord's own words will not escape earth's last judgments (Luke 21: 34-36).

"The spirit of a man is the lamp of the Lord" (Prov. 20: 27). In His parable of the virgins our Lord reveals there will be a lamp-trimming revival on the eve of His returning. How long does it take to trim a lamp? The wise have only time to trim their lamps, not fill them, before the door is closed. It is going to require constant, vigilant preparation of heart, life and lip to make and keep us ready to meet and greet our soul's Beloved when He, all glorious, comes to receive those "accepted in the Beloved."

"One known sin un-dropped, one known command disobeyed, one known truth unbelieved, one part of the life knowingly un-yielded, and we stand in jeopardy. The last shadows are falling across the world, and therefore across your life. Yet you are not ready; but there is time to win the victory before the sun goes down.

YOUR COMING JUDGE IS YOUR PRESENT SAVIOUR.
 Author
-The Midnight Cry.

Chapter One
Why Is Rapture Important

One area of major debate inside the Church is over the Second Coming and the Rapture of the Church. The debate centers around rapture being an invention of man, a false doctrine. Even those Christians who hold to a rapture often debate and differ in its timing. The positions which are most argued are 1) before the Tribulation, or 2) in the middle, or 3) at the end. While Charismatic Preterist teach the book of Revelation is 95% complete and there is not a rapture. In comparison to Premillennial teachers where the majority embrace Pre-Tribulation rapture. With smaller groups arguing for Mid Tribulation, or Post Tribulation rapture. Now Christians must consider all kinds of very good theologians differ on the timing of rapture doctrine. As the result Christians must study, and test the Spirit making decisions based upon the Word of God. Unfortunately, even with this study method the Church still holds different positions on the Rapture. With many fine Christian men and women holding to very diverse beliefs.

Now a very important question must be asked; "should I divide over my fellow brother in Christ over rapture doctrine?" In other words, should I have no fellowship with another Christian who believes in the rapture, and I do not? Or if I am a Pre-Tribulation rapture Christian, should I not fellowship with another brother in Christ who believes the rapture comes at Mid Tribulation or Post Tribulation? Also, should I then discredit another Christian theologian who holds to a different rapture belief than I do? Here is "my answer."

At different times in my walk with the Lord I have held different beliefs on the rapture. At first, I held the belief there was no rapture, and the Church would go all the way through the Tribulation and the be taken into the air (rapture) at the appearing of the Lord and resurrected into glory at the very end. I never understood those Christians who were looking to escape the Tribulation by rapture and considered them inferior Christians. I held a superiority attitude, and I thought myself more enlightened more developed than Christians who wanted to escape by Pre-Tribulation Rapture. I also held a doctrine called "Dominion Theology," which teaches the Church is transforming the world before the Second Coming of Jesus Christ. So, you can see how my "position" on the Second Coming was influenced by a Church conquering belief. I saw the Christian who wanted to escape the Tribulation as weak and holding a defeatist escapism mentality. However, I came to see Dominion Theology as fantasy, and a false doctrine. So now when I see Preterist teach Christians there is no Rapture and accuse those who hold to Rapture theology with an escape mentality, I understand. As those elitist attitudes exist among the Preterist are nothing new.

Today I understand more of the debate, and do not despise or divide over my brother in Christ over the Rapture. I trust the greater reality exists with the Rapture being connected to the Resurrection. If Christians hold to a future coming (Not 70 AD) of Jesus Christ, and a literal bodily resurrection of the saints called the first resurrection. Also, other important doctrines to consider from the Premillennial position is a Great Tribulation at the end of this age and the start of the next age called the Kingdom of Heaven (millennial kingdom). After the 1000-year reign of Christ the Kingdom of Heaven is delivered up to God the Father, and the New Heavens and New Earth begins. For me today the Rapture is about an "order to the Resurrection," which I understand many other good brothers and sisters in Christ disagree. In fact, I hold to a rapture position which very few in modern day Church would agree.

I hold to what is considered a selective rapture position, it is also a multiple rapture theology. Some of the Christian theologians which held and taught this position are: Watchman Née, G H Lang, George Peters, G H Pember, Joseph Seiss, Robert Govett and many others. Most of these men lived in the 1800's when the doctrine of the Millennial kingdom was being strongly taught and restored back into the Church. The selective rapture position teaches a thief like coming of the Lord to take only those saints who are watching and prayerful. With the rest of the saints who are sleeping and entangled with the world being left behind to experience a portion of the Tribulation trials. Only later to be raptured after suffering during a portion of the Great Tribulation and at the hands of the Antichrist. The selective rapture doctrine has a Pre-Tribulation, Mid Tribulation, and Post Tribulation rapture events. So, the selective rapture is also a multiple rapture belief. I trust "very few Christians" who hold to a literal rapture would hold to a selective rapture position. Most who believe in the rapture are Pre-Tribulation with the entire Church being removed at that time. Of course, those who hold to a no rapture position would certainly reject a multiple rapture position. I am currently writing on this subject bringing in teachings on selective rapture from those men like Watchman Nee who have taught this position extensively. I have been greatly influenced by Watchman Nee's teachings on other subjects, even if in the beginning I would have not agreed with his selective rapture position. This is my hope for modern day Christians will examine this doctrine and make a solid decision to prepare for the Second Coming of Jesus Christ.

Why is the rapture important? This would be a good question to consider as many modern-day Christians reject any belief in the catching away of the Church. So, let us consider ten significant facts related to the rapture which demonstrates its Biblical value.

1) Rapture demonstrates God's promise and provision.
2) Rapture shows an order to the Resurrection.
3) Rapture is given as a reward for faithful Christians.
4) Rapture is a sign of the Tribulation.
5) Rapture removes the saints to safety.
6) Rapture teaches the saints to watch and pray.
7) Rapture teaches the Church about spiritual warfare.
8) Rapture connects the saints with resurrection.
9) Rapture Is connected to the end of the age.
10) Rapture shows us the way into the Millennial Kingdom.
11) Rapture reveals the Bride of Christ.
12) Rapture ushers the saints into the Judgment Seat of Christ
13) Rapture teaches us to fear the wrath of God.
14) Rapture teaches of the Blessed Hope.
15) Rapture teaches Christians to love Christ's appearing.

The Growing Disdain for the Rapture

In the Charismatic Movement a growing trend towards disdaining the rapture is brought about by a belief in no rapture. Who is responsible for the increased putting down, and at times even mocking the rapture of the Church? The growing trend centers around Charismatic Christians who identify with the doctrine of Preterism.

In this teaching, Preterists believe Jesus Christ returned in 70 AD at the destruction of the Temple in Jerusalem. A Preterist believes the prophetic judgments of the Book of Revelation are all past, and no future judgments of God remain. So Preterism is diametrically opposed to the Pre-Millennial, Pre-Tribulation, and future rapture of the Church teaching. Christians must ask themselves why many Charismatics are jumping on the no rapture Preterist Bandwagon?"
You might say Charismatic Preterists do not believe in the supernatural, so taking Christians into the air in rapture at the coming of the Lord is laughable. However, I must protest if this is the argument because the Charismatic Preterist's are the signs and wonders crowd teaching we need to recover what the New Age stole from the Church. This is the same group which teaches, soul travel, speaking to the dead in heaven, and daily trips to the Throne of God in heaven. So, attempting to say Preterists cannot relate to the supernatural is not very reasonable. So, what is the main attraction? The answer is simple, Preterist's teach no future judgment, no future wrath of God.

Now the no Rapture Preterist crowd likes to view themselves as more optimistic. As compared to whom they call the "prophets of doom" who hold to a future coming Tribulation. Which is a silly argument, as the wrath of God is about the fear of the Lord, and not about an optimistic philosophy of improving the world. Was God not being optimistic when He destroyed the temple in 70 AD, and released His wrath as demonstrated in the Book of Revelation. Is there any time in history a Preterist can say any of Gods catastrophic judgments were optimistic? As optimism is a philosophy not a theology. The silly argument against a future Tribulation is really an attack on Gods judgments being perceived as negative. In the philosophical mind of Preterism a doom and gloomy end time picture. However, do not the judgments of God reveal the glory of the Lord? Where all of heaven praises God when His judgments fill the earth? The optimistic Preterist philosophy which teaches all judgments are past attack the Scriptural record of catastrophic end time judgments of God as recorded in the Bible. In this way Charismatic Preterists deny the coming rapture and base their optimistic philosophy on human wisdom and not Scriptural authority.

Now Charismatic Preterism accuses the Pretribulation rapture future wrath of God as an escape mentality. To which I reply, from what are Christians wanting to escape? The Preterist accuse the future rapture crowd of abandoning the world to the devil, and not fulfilling the Great Commission. To which I answer Preterism is only about 4% of the entire body of Christ worldwide. So, who has been doing most of the mission's work, obviously it is not been the Preterist's? In fact, the majority of Baptist Protestants who hold a Pre-Tribulation and Rapture theology are highly engaged in missions all over the world. The same goes for the

Charismatic Assemblies of God who hold to the same Pre-Tribulation and Rapture position. So once again the Preterist protest of an escape mentality using a false accusation. So, what does the rapture of the Church teach Christians must escape from?

The answer might be surprising to some Preterist's who have grown up on their eschatological beliefs, and that is all you ever were taught. The Rapture is about escaping the wrath of God. If you hold to the Pre-Millennial, Pre-Tribulation end time Rapture of the Church Gods end time judgments are released in the final years of this present evil age. The wrath of God is poured out over the entire world ending this age in catastrophic judgments. The wrath of God will be against a world who has forsaken God, denied Jesus Christ, the Cross, and the Resurrection of Jesus Christ.

Instead, the nations of the earth rise to take the Mark of the Beast and worship the Antichrist as God. The wrath of God is revealed against all men who suppress the truth in unrighteousness and are natural enemies to God. Children of wrath, and sons of disobedience. As anyone can really see by Scriptures the wrath of God still abides upon all men who refuse Jesus Christ. God's end time judgments are not fulfilled and are not complete and will be finalized at the Second Coming. The final judgments of God are recorded in the Book of Revelation and are the outpouring of God's end time wrath.

So, the escape mentality of Pre-Tribulation Christians is not a flight from responsibility, or the devil, and instead is an escape into safety. Who does the rapture protect? Christians who are alive during the time of God's out pouring of wrath all over the world. The Rapture is a supernatural catching up of watchful and praying Christians who are looking for God's protection. Escape is possible by rapture as the catastrophic judgments shake the heavens and the earth.

The rapture of the Church is another way God demonstrates His mercy and grace. The faithful saint is removed from end time catastrophic events in order to be protected by God and to escape from the persecution of the Antichrist. In this way is the Rapture is an action of God's saving grace and mercy. The Rapture is God's way of escape for watchful saints who are alive at the time of the Tribulation. Yes, the faithful are removed by God into His shelter in the sky where they will abide in the "shadow of the Almighty," until God's wrath is finalized in the heavens and earth.

(1 Thessalonians 4:13-18) 1
13 But I would not have you to be
ignorant, brethren, concerning them which are
asleep, that ye sorrow not, even as others which
have no hope.
14 For if we believe that Jesus died and rose again, even so them also which sleep in Jesus will God

bring with him.
15 For this we say unto you by the word of the Lord, that we which are alive and remain unto the coming of the Lord shall not prevent them which are asleep.
16 For the Lord himself shall descend from heaven with a shout, with the voice of the archangel, and with the trump of God: and the dead in Christ shall rise first:
17 Then we which are alive and remain shall be caught up together with them in the clouds, to meet the Lord in the air: and so shall we ever be with the Lord.
18 Wherefore comfort one another with these words.

In case you do not understand the Preterist agenda, Preterist preach the Book of Revelation as a history lesson. In Preterist philosophy the prophetic judgments of the book of Revelation have already happened in history. You can tell a Charismatic Preterist by their insistence on no future Antichrist, no coming dark days of Tribulation, no Great Falling Away of the Church, and no rapture. Preterist's holding these philosophical beliefs in mind, sets out to attack Bible Scriptures on the Rapture.

What is their point of attack, not that it (rapture) ever happened in history (as it never has), instead Preterist attack the purpose of the rapture? Preterists teach rapture is an escape from responsibility. Preterist see the mission of the Church to transform the world before Jesus Christ can return. The attack on the rapture by Charismatic Preterist rests on their belief it is an escape and hands the devil the world by default. However, is this a true picture of how the Bible teaches the catching up of the Church at the Second Coming of the Lord?

1) Is Rapture an escape according to Scriptures? The answer is yes. However, it is an escape into refuge into safety, and into God's protection. It is not a running away from responsibility as no man can rapture himself. It is God's way of preserving the righteous while His wrath is being poured out upon the wicked worldwide. It is Gods way of preparing an ark of refuge. Noah was given an Ark which took him above the flood waters of Gods wrath preserving Noah and his family for a new age on earth. The wicked were destroyed below by the flood while the eight souls of Noah and family were kept in refuge. In safety and protected above the flood water of God's judgment on earth.

   Rapture is not an act of irresponsibility and flight instead it is an act of righteous obedience. Without faith and obedience Noah would have not taken the Lords warning of coming worldwide catastrophic judgment and made preparation. It is the same for those who are looking for the rapture in watchfulness and prayer. A walk of faith and obedience in a time when lawlessness is abounding. In a time when the world and many in the Church mock catastrophic age ending judgment of Gods wrath.

2) The rapture is not an escape instead it is a removal by God of the righteous not the wicked. The Bible teaches it is the righteous which are taken into the clouds not the wicked. What happens to the wicked? The nations which refuse the council of God are turned into Hell. The grapes of wrath are kept in store for the great wine press of the wrath of God Almighty. The Prettiest have lost sight of Gods righteous indignation. How loving is a God who will drown men by a great deluge of water saving only eight men alive? In the no judgment Charismatic theological grid there is only room for a lovey dovey patronizing papa God that does not have one once of wrath left in Him.

Let us get this straight. Why does God have to remove the righteous in rapture? His wrath is being poured out on the wicked, and the earth is not a safe place to remain. This is not a flight from responsibility, it is a flight from Gods destroying wrath. The Preterist are blinded from the wrath to come. Without a Biblical view of Gods coming wrath, you cannot tell if God is a jolly old Santa Clause, or Jesus Christ the Lord God who sits on the Throne.

The judgment of God is being completely removed by an antichrist spirit in these days. The Charismatic Preterist have taken the bait and are become the false messengers of "peace, peace." The Charismatics are putting the Church asleep by not preparing saints to stand in watch and prayer. Standing against end time apostasy and deception. Instead Preterist are attacking the Scriptures which demonstrate an end time Tribulation, and the final outpouring of Gods wrath.

The Christian No Judgment Generation

What happens when you remove all judgment out from the Christian faith? What happens when the Church and the world send out the same message; who are you to judge me? The rising popularity in the Preterist Charismatic Movement teaches all judgment is past, and the Book of Revelation is 95% complete. Also, the Charismatic Preterist crowd teach a worldwide Church take over. Have mocked Christians who warn of end time judgments calling them prophets of doom. Where have Christians come when Christians believe only the love of God without judgment remains?

Truthfully speaking this is one of the most incredibly dangerous positions any person, not just Christians can enter. To prove the extent of the deception, many

Preterist teachers often promote some form of Universal Salvation. An ancient heresy which teaches all men will be saved out of Hell. In the similar way the world believes in no consequences for sin. The unsaved world simply believes if you just believe in God, you die and go to heaven. What then is the world's attitude before the Second Coming, and on the final judgments of God's wrath? It will be as in the days of Noah, marrying and given in marriage, buying and selling, and carrying on with their own deceived existences as if the world were never going to end.

All this not believing in God's wrath and judgment had become popular in the world right before the flood, which destroyed them all. Only Noah and his family took seriously the warnings of the coming flood of God's wrath and made preparation to escape. Now was Noah mocked and scorned for his actions, and was Noah treated as a prophet of doom? Sadly, the Bible predicts the same attitude towards the coming wrath of God in the last days. Similar attitudes towards God's wrath and judgment will be as in the days of Noah. Sadly, also the Bible predicts a Great Falling Away from the faith when Christians will be like the world. An end time Laodicean Church who has the world's goods but has shut out God and are blinded to the end time judgments of God.

Will their mockery and unbelief towards the end time wrath and judgments of God reduce what the Bible has warned? Let us let the apostle Peter teach the Church

about this temptation. "Knowing this first, that there shall come in the last days scoffers, walking after their own lusts, and saying where is the promise of His coming? For since the father fell asleep (history of humanity), all things continues they the way they were from the beginning of creation."
(2 Peter 3:3-4) 2

The apostle Peter explains they are "willing ignorant," which means they agree with deception, not wanting to remember how God judged the entire world before with the great flood of Noah. Also close their eyes and ears not wanting to know about how God teaches of another end time judgment. Where the heavens and earth which are now are kept in store reserved for fire of God's wrath which is sealed now, but soon to be released. Happens at the end of the age called the Day of the Lord, the day of Judgment and destruction of ungodly men. Also, the escape of the righteous prayerful saints into the clouds, a removal from harm's way.

For in a time where mankind is saying peace and safety comes the sudden destruction of the Lord. For the Day of the Lord will come as a thief in the night in which the heavens will pass away with a great noise, and the elements shall melt with fervent heat. Will Christians who are serious in their relationship with Jesus Christ taking the Word of God their final authority, say, "all this judgment is already past?" Is evidence inside the

Church of scoffing and mocking future judgments as Scriptures warn Christians will be tempted in the last days? Has the earth and all it is works been burned up by the wrath and end time judgments of God? Does anyone really believe the world has already been judged as described in the Bible? (2 Peter 3:10)

Now one final thought for the Christian's to consider in teaching all judgment has already passed. Is Preterist philosophy leading the Church more like the Church of Philadelphia? Philadelphian Christians we are commended by Jesus Christ for their Christ likeness. In living like Jesus Christ by picking up the Cross in self-denial, and crucified to the world? Or are the Preterist leading the saints into blindness as rebuked by Jesus Christ. A modern day Preterist Church more like Laodicean Christians who are blind, wretched, and naked, having accumulated the world's goods and calling their worldliness the "blessing of God?"

The Church of the first century was dying for their faith looking for the coming Day of the Lord, and a better resurrection. The Charismatic Preterist teach the day of the Lord has already come and all judgment is past, and the first resurrection is to be assumed, spiritually of course. Are Preterist beliefs leading Christians to the Laodicean Church who looks like the world lives like the world, and mocks the judgments of the Second Coming? Now for those who refuse to live the Laodicean Church age and fearing the Coming Day of the Lord take this warning seriously: "You therefore, beloved, seeing ye know these things before, beware lest ye also, being led away with the error of the wicked, fall from your own steadfastness." (2 Peter 3:17) (3)

How Would You React to Noah's Warning?

So, you live in the days of Noah, a mad man building a three-tier boat as big as a football field on dry land. The reason Noah is taking on such an enormous lifetime task is he is afraid of God's coming judgment. Let us see what Scriptures say about Noah's response to God when being warned about God's coming judgment of flood waters.
Hebrews 11:6-7 (4)
6 But without faith it is impossible to please him: for he that cometh to God must believe that he is, and that he is a rewarder of them that diligently seek him.
7 By faith Noah, being warned of
God of things not seen as yet, moved with
fear, prepared an ark to the saving of his house; by the which he condemned the world, and became heir of the righteousness which is by faith.

Noah was warned of God of things not seen yet, and he became very afraid. Why, because Noah took God at His word, and prepared for the coming catastrophic judgments. Now the Book of Revelation warns of the coming end time catastrophic judgments which shall end this present evil age. Christians in the same way are to respond to God's warning with the fear of the Lord. Responding with faith requires the saints to understand God is not going to save the world. Instead, the world which is now is been kept in store for God's fire. The earth is going to burn with the fire of God's judgment where in the elements of the heaven and earth will melt with fervent heat.

What will be the attitude in the earth concerning the coming catastrophic ending of this present evil age? The Scriptures inform as it will be the same as the days of Noah. People will be buying and selling, marrying and given in marriage until the flood came and took them all away. In the time right before the great deluge of waters in Noah's day people were living as if the world would never end. Now God (Jesus Christ) had great wrath against the Noah's generation as the world was filled with violence, and the thought of man was continuously evil. (Genesis 6:5&11) Did men fear the words of Noah? Did men take serious how Noah and his family spent their whole lives preparing for the coming judgment?

The answer lies in the facts, mankind had lost all fear of the Lord. Only Noah and his family had the capacity to take seriously the warning of impending catastrophic judgment. Not that evidence of impending judgment was not clear, as the signs of God's sovereignty were demonstrated by events like when the animals were gathered into the Ark.

Now the Scriptures warn in our days the condition which existed before Noah's Great Flood will happen again. Mankind will have lost all fear the Lord and will mock God's judgment, and Second Coming. Knowing in the last days scoffers will come walking after their own lusts, saying "where is the promise of His coming?" In other words, we do not believe it, it has been this way from the very beginning. With Christians who are taught all judgment is past wrongly believe a loving God would never send humanity to an eternal hell fire. For those who have outsmarted God inside the Church, they will be tempted to simply mock the coming catastrophic judgments by saying all judgment is already past. As for what Preterist teach instead of a future catastrophic Tribulation is a coming Christian Utopia on earth before Jesus Christ can return.

What is truly alarming is the numbers of Christians who are mocking the Christians who are warning of the coming judgment of God. Foolishly accusing Christians who teach a future Tribulation, saying to those who hold this position you are prophets of doom, or a Pharisee, or a legalist living under the law. In this culture of unbelief how many Christians are watching and praying watching to escape? Watching and praying the way the Lord Jesus Christ has warned? How many are not married to the world, and are continuing as a sojourner knowing this present age is not their home? How many will not be prepared at the thief in the night coming of the Lord, where one will be taken the other left behind? How many saints will miss the Pre-Tribulation Rapture, and face the Tribulation? A time where Jesus Christ the opens the Seven Sealed Book of end time judgments. Releasing the four horsemen of the apocalypse in catastrophic Judgments, and leading to the appearing of the Antichrist? (2 Peter 3:3-14)

Resurrection and Rapture

Have you noticed how little Christians put their hope in the Second Coming as the place of transformation? Most modern-day culture put glorification of a man's life after they die, and then automatically placing them in heaven and in glory. However, death is treated as an enemy by Scriptures a separation of soul from the body into a disembodied state of death. It is not glorification, as if glorification where outside the human body. Instead, glorification is related to the rejoining of the soul with your body at the Second Coming and the First Resurrection of the righteous dead.

Sadly, many men will deny their need to be saved out from among the dead, and wrongly believe they are automatically awarded heaven and glory upon their death. Instead, those who have refused Jesus Christ descend into Hell upon their death their soul being tormented in Hell fire, and their body returning to the earth from which it has been made.

Now the Bible teaches both resurrection and rapture. For the dead in Christ will be raised out from among the dead, and the living in Christ will be raised up from the earth into the clouds into the sky. The Scriptures are exact and clear both these events must occur for the salvation of the body of Christians transforming them from mortality into immortality. The problem has arisen in the Church when spirit glorification is taught, and death has glorified a man in a spiritual state. However, that doctrine does not exist in the Christian faith.

Glorification is not related to this age as our mortality is the result of sin and death. Glorification is not availed until the Second Coming. A false glory is being taught today as Christians are said to glorified now in Christ in our heavenly position. It is a false doctrine, a denial of our mortality, and the glorification upon resurrection. Being glorified from our mortality into immorality at the time of Resurrection and Rapture is the true doctrine of Scriptures.

Attacking or denying the rapture is an attack on the plan of salvation and the Second Coming. It has become popular to downplay or deny the rapture. It is excused as unbelief and escapism, however, just the opposite is true as the whole of the Christian faith is based upon the Resurrection.
The dead in Christ are raised first then those who are alive and remain are taken from the earth without death into the clouds of the sky. Where is the Church

gathered unto the Lord? Both the dead in Christ being raised from the dead, and the living in Christ rise from the earth to meet the Lord in the clouds. Dare any man teach there is no rapture, or it is an escape mentality? Instead, it is the promise of the blessed hope for without our Resurrection and Rapture there is no salvation of the body.

Attacking the rapture is to deny the process of salvation. The Charismatic Preterist who teaches a worldwide take over downplays or denies the significance of the Rapture. The reason why? They teach "spirit glorification," much like a New Age man which is evolving into a divine being. The Charismatic Preterist Movement is caught up into these New Age beliefs teaching the false doctrine of the Manifested Sons of God. Teaching the Church at the end of the Age will be filled with the Divinity of Christ, and Christ will first bring His glorification through the Church before He can return in the Second Coming. This heresy is like the New Age beliefs of a corporate divine man who is evolving to transform the world into a golden age of Aquarius.

Watch out for any man which denies the significance of Resurrection and Rapture as they are promoting some concept of man's glorification. Without the Biblical process of transformation from mortality into immortality. "Behold, I shew you a mystery; We shall not all sleep, but we shall all be changed, in a moment, in the twinkling of an eye, at the last trump: for the

trumpet shall sound, and the dead shall be raised incorruptible, and we shall be changed."
(1 Corinthians 15:51) (5)

1 Corinthians 15:35-58 (6)
35 But some man will say, how are the dead raised up? and with what body do they come?
36 Thou fool, that which thou sowest is not quickened, except it die:
37 And that which thou sowest, thou sowest not that body that shall be, but bare grain, it may chance of wheat, or of some other grain:
38 But God giveth it a body as it hath pleased him, and to every seed his own body.
39 All flesh is not the same flesh: but there is one kind of flesh of men, another flesh of beasts, another of fishes, and another of birds.
40 There are also celestial bodies, and bodies terrestrial: but the glory of the celestial is one, and the glory of the terrestrial is another.
41 There is one glory of the sun, and another glory of the moon, and another glory of the stars: for one-star differeth from another star in glory.
42 So also is the resurrection of the dead. It is sown in corruption; it is raised in incorruption:
43 It is sown in dishonour; it is raised in glory: it is sown in weakness; it is raised in power:
44 It is sown a natural body; it is raised a spiritual body. There is a natural body, and there is a spiritual body.

45 And so it is written, the first man Adam was made a living soul; the last Adam was made a quickening spirit.
46 Howbeit that was not first which is spiritual, but that which is natural; and afterward that which is spiritual.
47 The first man is of the earth, earthy: the second man is the Lord from heaven. 48 As is the earthy, such are they also that are earthy: and as is the heavenly, such are they also that are heavenly.
49 And as we have borne the image of the earthy, we shall also bear the image of the heavenly.
50 Now this I say, brethren, that flesh and blood cannot inherit the kingdom of God; neither doth corruption inherit incorruption.
51 Behold, I shew you a mystery; We shall not all sleep, but we shall all be changed,
52 In a moment, in the twinkling of an eye, at the last trump: for the trumpet shall sound, and the dead shall be raised incorruptible, and we shall be changed.
53 For this corruptible must put on incorruption, and this mortal must put on immortality.
54 So when this corruptible shall have put on incorruption, and this mortal shall have put on immortality, then shall be brought to pass the saying that is written, Death is swallowed up in victory.
55 O death, where is thy sting? O grave, where is thy victory?
56 The sting of death is sin; and the strength of sin is the law.
57 But thanks be to God, which giveth us the victory through our Lord Jesus Christ.

58 Therefore, my beloved brethren, be ye stedfast, unmovable, always abounding in the work of the Lord, forasmuch as ye know that your labour is not in vain in the Lord.

Chapter 2
What is the Rapture?

Technically speaking the term rapture cannot be found in the Bible. Nowhere in all of Scriptures can the word rapture be found. On this technicality alone many Christians want to say it is not Biblical to believe in the rapture. However, it is not quite that easy to dismiss the principle of the rapture because the actual word does not appear in Scriptures. If that be the case, we would have to eliminate the doctrine of the Trinity because that word Trinity does not actually appear in the Bible either. So sometimes Christian concepts are given as Scriptural principles like Trinity, meaning the Father, Son, Holy Spirit the three persons of the Godhead in order to describe Bible terms. This is what the word rapture is like, it is a description of an event which occurs at the Second Coming of the Lord. Rapture is the doctrine where the Church is taken before or during the time of Tribulation up into the clouds by a supernatural gathering of the Lord. Probably one of the clearest Scriptures of the Church being raptured into the clouds is found in the apostle Paul's letter to the Church of Thessalonians.

1 Thessalonians 4:13-18 (7)
13 But I would not have you to be
ignorant, brethren, concerning them which are
asleep, that ye sorrow not, even as others which
have no hope.
14 For if we believe that Jesus died and rose again, even
so them also which sleep in Jesus will God
bring with him.
15 For this we say unto you by the word of the
Lord, that we which are alive and remain unto the
coming of the Lord shall not prevent them which are
asleep.
16 For the Lord himself shall
descend from heaven with a shout, with the voice of the
archangel, and with the trump of God: and the
dead in Christ shall rise first:
17 Then we which are alive and remain shall be caught
up together with them in the clouds, to meet the
Lord in the air: and so shall we ever be with the Lord.
18 Wherefore comfort one another with these words.

Notice the context is the Second Coming of the Lord, and the Church both the dead in Christ and those which are alive at the Lord's coming. Are caught up together to meet the Lord in the clouds. There is no denying the actual gathering of the Church is a rapture into the clouds. So, the only real argument only exists in the timing of the event, not wither or not it will happen.

The rapture is completely Biblical proven by many Scriptures which all confirm the same thing. A catching up of the saints into the clouds meeting the Lord at His coming. Scripture after Scripture confirms a supernatural taking from the earth, or from the realm of the dead. Saints of old coming out of their graves and living Christians into the clouds of the sky to meet the descending presence of the Lord out of heaven.

No real student of Bible, theologians, or scholars can deny the events of the rapture. Many Christian teachers attempt to teach against a Pre-Tribulation rapture of the Church, saying the rapture itself is just one big event. At the Second Coming of the Lord where the saints are raised from mortality to immortality. The resurrection and the rapture are just the same event with no time lapse in between. In comparison, Christians who teach on a Pre-Tribulation rapture place a space of time between the rapture, and final resurrection of the righteous dead.

We can see the majority of Rapture Christians do not argue the point of being taken into the sky at the Second Coming. Some say rapture with many years delay before the actual coming, others rapture without delay before the Second Coming and the resurrection of the righteous. While others speak of multiple raptures one before, one in the middle, and one at the end of the Tribulation.

The apostle Paul lists the order of events of the Church being taken; first the dead in Christ, and those who are alive and remain when the Lord descends out of Heaven. The descending of the Lord from out of heaven's Throne Room is accompanied by the shout of the archangel, and the sounding of the Trumpet of God. In this Scripture Paul does not say if it is the last trumpet of God, or some other only that God's trumpet will sound. When these events are set into motion, the Lord does not at this time descend all the way to earth, instead the saints both the dead and the living rise to meet the Lord in the air. The order of taking is the dead in Christ rise first, then the living saints are taken and are caught up alive together with the Lord in the clouds.

Now it is very important to understand from that time the saints both those formerly dead, and those who were taken alive will remain with the Lord forever. So, we must consider the rapture and resurrection cannot be disconnected. The rapture is clearly positioned at the Second Coming of Jesus Christ so has never occurred at any time in history before. Instead, the rapture of the Church points to the Second Coming and the first resurrection of the righteous dead and living.

So, the technical aspect of the rapture is a supernatural catching up of the Church both the dead and living into the clouds to ever be with the Lord. Obviously, this event has never happened at any time in history and will not happen until the Lord descends from His throne in the clouds of the sky. Many teach the rapture of the Church into the first resurrection as a reward for faithful saints who qualify by righteous living. No non-Christians, no unbelievers will take part in the rapture, or the first resurrection.

No man can say the rapture has already happened as a spiritual event, like the resurrection is already past. This puts the Preterists who teach Jesus Christ returned in 70 AD at odds with Scripture, so they must deny the rapture with their false doctrine. To spiritualize the rapture or the resurrection placing those events at any time in history is simply heretical teaching.

No man can say he knows the time of the rapture either. For the rapture is connected to the first resurrection and the Second Coming of Jesus Christ. So Christian fanatical teachers who are always setting the date of the Lord's rapture and second Coming are just blowing hot smoke. They do not know what time, the day or the hour, as it is having not been given for any man to know. So, the date setters and prognosticators have brought a great reproach on the authority of Scriptures and have drawn the mockery from all their failed predictions. Both inside and outside the Church. So, it is not for Christians to know the date of the rapture, the first resurrection, or the Lord's return. Only, that we must keep our eyes wide open, and watch and pray always setting the hope of the Lord's return before us.

Now that we can see those who attempt to refute the rapture are wrong, and those who attempt to predict its date are wrong. Let us investigate what would be the right Scriptural position and attitude about the doctrine of the catching up of the Church. For the sake of writing this thesis, I will simply say "rapture, "even though the word is not directly written in the Bible is evidenced in sound doctrine by Scriptures. However, having discussed the reason why rapture removes watchful praying Christians, let us move forward with the Scriptural evidence. Also, the record Church history and statements from Church forefathers. Also reviewing development of the rapture doctrine in the past 1800 plus years. For we know there has been a long delay between the first coming of the Lord, and the Second Coming. So many leaders and teachers inside the Church have either approved or disapproved of the rapture. As to the Pre-Tribulation and Pre-Millennial doctrine of the Church the events of the rapture and resurrection are still future. This one thing Pre-Millennialism I can say about its timing.

Chapter 3
Why Is There A Debate Over the Rapture?

A modern debate has arisen among Christians, teaching there is no rapture, or just a resurrection without a rapture. I guess the first reason would be an overall ignorance concerning the events of the Second Coming.

The Book of Revelation records the Second Coming of Jesus Christ in detail, but simply put many pastors are afraid to teach the Book. Or like Preterist, put a historical spin on the Book of Revelation and say the prophetic events all occurred in 70 AD. They attempt to rid the Church of the rapture all together. A modern debate has arisen among Christians, teaching there is no rapture, or just a resurrection without a rapture.

However, a large portion of the Church holds to a Pre-Tribulation rapture doctrinal position which has made the series of books and movies entitled; "Left Behind" quite popular. Movies and books made for Left Behind show Christians disappearing while driving cars, or while flying in airplanes making for quite sensational scenes. However, I am not convinced it is teaching the Biblical narrative of the rapture accurately. It is true in times past the popularity of a Pre-Tribulation rapture sold books and movies tickets and even made some Christians a good deal of money. However, today the Pre-Tribulation rapture is losing ground in the Church and its viability is being called into question.

Now we have to ask ourselves why in the 1800's did the doctrine of the rapture gain new recognition and respect? While today Christians make fun and even mock the notion of an end time rapture of the Church. What has changed in the last two hundred years to move the Church away from a catastrophic Second

Coming and the rapture of prayerful watching Christians?

Dominion Theology

Part of the answer is in the rise of theological positions which teach against the coming millennial kingdom and a Tribulation at the end of this age. In the Charismatic Church two eschatology's which support this view are growing in popularity. One is called Post Millennialism, and the other called Preterism. In the Charismatic world both position basically state the judgments of God are past and only a Golden Age of the Church remains.

In the Charismatic Post Millennial view the Church is thought to be the Kingdom of Heaven on earth right now. As the millennial began with the first coming of Jesus Christ and the outpouring of the Holy Spirit on the day of Pentecost. There are other versions of the Post Millennial view, but basically the Church is taught the millennial kingdom is now, and the Kingdom of Heaven is expanding all over the world by the Church. In the end after the whole world has been Christianized by the Church and Christian Utopian millennial conditions exists on earth among the nations. Jesus Christ can then return, and the Church will hand the Kingdom over to the Lord at that time.

In Charismatic Theology this doctrine is called "Kingdom Now," as the Church is viewed as the Kingdom of heaven on earth and in the Millennium now. Connected to the Kingdom Now Post Millennial Position is a doctrine called Dominion Theology. Which teaches Jesus Christ has restored to the Church the dominion Adam lost to Satan in the Garden of Eden. The Kingdom Now/Dominion Theology doctrine is growing in popularity among Charismatics. Charismatic Dominion Theology also teach a restored government of apostles and prophets who will spread the proper Church government all over the world. This Apostolic and Prophetic government goes by the name of the New Apostolic Reformation, or NAR for short. The NAR is the source of many Post Millennial and Preterist Charismatics Christians. Here is a brief description of the Kingdom Now Dominionism Church:

"Kingdom Now theology is a branch of Dominion Theology which has had a following
within Pentecostalism. It attracted attention in the late 1980s.[23][24]
Kingdom Now theology states that although Satan has been in control of the world since the Fall, God is looking for people who will help him take back dominion. Those who yield themselves to the authority of God's apostles and prophets will take control of the kingdoms of this world, being defined as all social institutions, the "kingdom" of education, the "kingdom" of science, the "kingdom" of the arts, etc.[25] C. Peter Wagner, the founder of the New Apostolic Reformation, writes: "The practical theology that best builds a

foundation under social transformation is dominion theology, sometimes called 'Kingdom Now.' Its history can be traced back through R. J. Rushdoony and Abraham Kuyper to John Calvin."[26]

Kingdom Now theology is influenced by the Latter Rain movement,[27] and critics have connected it to the New Apostolic Reformation,[28] "Spiritual Warfare Christianity,"[27] and Fivefold ministry thinking.[29]" (Wikipedia) 8

What is the major shift in end time theology with the Kingdom Now/ Dominion Theology Charismatic Church? The basic difference is how the Church will take over the world by Christianizing the nations before Jesus Christ can return. Now one major difference between the Pre-Tribulation and Pre-Millennial position, is Kingdom Now teaches the prophetic judgments of the Book of Revelation already past in history. So, without any future catastrophic judgments the Charismatic Church can now effectually take over the world. The Preterist golden age of the Millennium is now. Satan's dominion has been lost to the Church, and the Dominion given to the Charismatic Church can now overthrow the Satanic systems which hold humanity captive. The popularity of Kingdom Now Dominion Theology teaches a worldwide take over and purging of culture. Charismatic Dominion Theology also goes by the name called the 7 Mountain Gospel.

Here is an excerpt:
The Seven Mountain Gospel or the seven-mountain prophecy is an anti-biblical and damaging movement that has gained a following in some Charismatic and Pentecostal churches. Those who follow the seven-mountain mandate believe that, for Christ to return to earth, the church must take control of the seven major spheres of influence in society for the glory of Christ. Once the world has been made subject to the kingdom of God, Jesus will return and rule the world.
Here are the seven mountains, according to the seven-mountain mandate:
1) Education 2) Religion 3) Family 4) Business 5) Government/Military 6) Arts/Entertainment 7) Media
These seven sectors of society are thought to mold the way everyone thinks and behaves. So, to tackle societal change, these seven mountains must be transformed. The mountains are also referred to as "pillars, shapers, molders, and spheres." Those who follow the seven-mountain mandate speak of occupying the mountains, invading the culture, and transforming society.

The seven mountain mandate has its roots in dominion theology, which started in the early 1970s with a goal of "taking dominion" of the earth, twisting Genesis 1:28 to include a mandate for Christians to control civil affairs and all other aspects of society. The New Apostolic Reformation, with its self-appointed prophets and apostles, has also influenced the seven mountain movement, lending dreams and visions and other extra-

biblical revelations to the mandate.
The seven mountain mandate says that it is the duty of all Christians to create a worldwide kingdom for the glory of Christ. Teachers in the movement use Isaiah 2:2, which mentions mountains, in an attempt to support their view: "In the last days the mountain of the LORD's temple will be established as the highest of the mountains; it will be exalted above the hills, and all nations will stream to it." The principal goal of dominion theology and the seven-mountain mandate is political and religious domination of the world through the implementation of the moral laws—and subsequent punishments—of the Old Testament."

https://www.gotquestions.org/seven-mountain-mandate.html (9)

Let us think about this major shift in end time eschatological view which has accelerated in the last twenty years. From a coming pre wrath, pre-Tribulation catastrophic ending, instead shifting to a worldwide Church take over. As the result of no future Tribulation Post Millennials' see no need for a rapture of the Church to be removed from God's coming wrath. Kingdom Now Theology has this philosophy, if God is not going to judge the world anymore, and no future judgments remain the only conclusion is for a Charismatic Church Golden Age. Why have a rapture of the Church been taking over the world?

The other group which holds to the Kingdom Now/Dominion theology Charismatic position, are Preterist, or partial Preterist. The basic belief of Preterism is Jesus Christ returned in 70 AD in the destruction of the temple in Jerusalem, and the prophetic judgments of the Book of Revelation were fulfilled at that time.

"Preterism is a Christian eschatological view that interprets some (partial Preterism) or all (full Preterism) prophecies of the Bible as events which have already happened. This school of thought interprets the Book of Daniel as referring to events that happened in the 2nd century BC, while seeing the prophecies of Revelation as events that happened in the first century AD. Preterism holds that Ancient Israel finds its continuation or fulfillment in the Christian church at the destruction of Jerusalem in AD 70.
The term Preterism comes from the Latin praetor, which Webster's 1913 dictionary lists as a prefix denoting that something is "past" or "beyond". Adherents of Preterism are commonly known as preterists. Preterism teaches that either all (full Preterism) or a majority (partial Preterism) of the Olivet discourse had come to pass by AD 70.
Historically, preterists and non-preterists have generally agreed that the Jesuit Luis de Alcasar (1554–1613) wrote the first systematic preterist exposition of prophecy - Vestigatio arcani sensus in

45

Apocalypsi (published in 1614)—during the Counter-Reformation." (Wikipedia) 10

One might now understand just from an eschatological standpoint why Post Millennial and Preterist Charismatics so attack the doctrine of Pretribulation and Rapture theology. All this goes against the Preterist 70 AD fulfillment of the prophetic judgments of the Book of Revelation. As the position of Post Millennial is in 180 degrees complete opposition to Pre-Millennial, Pre-Tribulation eschatology. Post Millennial theology leads Christians to deny the rapture as Christian mythology.

Charismatic Christians who are jumping on board with Preterist and Post Millennial eschatology are tempted to mock the purpose of the Rapture. Why believe in the foolishness of a supernatural catching up of the Church when none is absolutely needed?

What is also obvious is no middle ground exists between these eschatological positions. Charismatic Preterists have the prophetic catastrophic judgments of God in the past, while the Pre-Tribulation position is still looking for the future coming Tribulation. The catastrophic judgments of God at the end of this present age. The net effect is a complete opposite in terms of the Second Coming.

One thing is for sure both positions cannot be right. Christians must make the choice is all judgment already past in history, yes or no? Many Charismatic's have sided with the Post Millennial and Preterist past judgment theories. However, the contents of this book will prove the Pre-Millennial and Pre-Tribulation is the one with the testimony of Scripture. With this end time view in place, the Church can see the necessity of an end time Rapture(s) of the saints.

Chapter 4
Darby and Dispensationalism

Who is John Darby and what is Dispensationalism? Also, why do the Preterist's attack Mr. Darby to prove their doctrine of Kingdom Now/Dominion Theology? John Darby would be considered the most familiar face of an historical Christian teacher who espoused the doctrines of Pre-Millennialism, Pre-Tribulation, and the rapture of the saints. So, everything John Darby teaches about the Second Coming of Jesus Christ would be a contradiction to Preterism. So, the Preterist spend a lot of time attempting to prove the Rapture, and Dispensational Pre-Millennialism is a manmade invention which has originated with John Darby and was never held by the Church before him.

"John Nelson Darby (18 November 1800 – 29 April 1882) was an Anglo-Irish Bible teacher, one of the influential figures among the original Plymouth Brethren and the founder of the Exclusive Brethren. He is considered to be the father of modern Dispensationalism and Futurism. Pre-tribulation rapture theology was popularized extensively in the 1830s by John Nelson Darby and the Plymouth Brethren,[1] and further popularized in the United States in the early 20th century by the wide circulation of the Scofield Reference Bible." (Wikipedia) 11

Darby developed a systematic approach to how God dealt with people before the formation of the Church. This systematic approach to different periods of history in which John Darby is accredited is called "Dispensationalism."

"Dispensationalists are premillennialists who affirm a future, literal 1,000-year reign of Jesus Christ which merges with and continues on to the eternal state in the "new heavens and the new earth",[18] and they claim that the millennial kingdom will be theocratic in nature and not mainly soteriological, as it is considered by George Eldon Ladd and others with a non-dispensational form of premillennialism.
Dispensationalism is known for its opinions respecting the nation of Israel during this millennial kingdom reign, in which Israel as a nation plays a major role and regains a king, a land, and an everlasting kingdom.
The vast majority of dispensationalists profess the Pretribulation rapture, with small minorities professing to either a mid-tribulation or post-tribulation rapture." (Wikipedia) 12

As you can see by the very nature of dispensational beliefs the eschatology is Premillennial and Pre-Tribulation which a point to future judgments, and not history. You can see why Preterist want to do everything in their power to discredit dispensational teaching. So, we must ask three basic questions 1) Did the teaching on a future millennial kingdom exist before John Darby 2) Did the teaching on and end time Tribulation exist before John Darby and 3) Did the teaching on the catching up of the saints into the clouds exist before John Darby?

The reason Christians need to ask those three questions is to find out what the early Church fathers believed about the Rapture and the coming millennial kingdom age. If they held the position before John Darby how far back does this teaching on Pre-Millennial, Pre-Tribulation, and the catching up of the saints into the sky really go? Does it go back to the first century Church, or even to the time of the teaching of the original apostles? To answer these questions let us quote from well know Church Father is of history.

What was the first century Church position on the millennium? Before or after the Second Coming of Jesus Christ? Were first century Christians Pre Millennial or Post Millennial or A Millennial (no millennial age). This might surprise many Charismatics who sold out to the Preterist position, but for the first two hundred years of the Christian faith the Church was "exclusively Pre-Millennial."

"The doctrine of Premillennialism has strong support in church history. In fact, Premillennialism was the prevailing millennial view for the first 300 years of church history. As the historian Philip Schaff states, "The most striking point in the eschatology of the ante-Nicene age is the prominent chiliasm, or millenarianism, that is the belief of a visible reign of Christ in glory on earth with the risen saints for a thousand years, before the general resurrection and judgment".
(Philip Schaff, History of the Christian Church, 2:614) 13

"Justin Martyr in the 2nd century was one of the first Christian writers to clearly describe himself as continuing in the "Jewish" belief of a temporary messianic kingdom prior to the eternal state. According to Johannes Quasten, "In his eschatological ideas Justin shares the views of the Chiliasts concerning the millennium He maintains a premillennial distinctive, namely that there would be two resurrections, one of believers before Jesus' reign and then a general resurrection afterwards. Justin wrote in chapter 80 of his work Dialogue with Trypho, "I and others who are right-minded Christians on all points are assured that there will be a resurrection of the dead, and a thousand years in Jerusalem, which will then be built... For Isaiah spoke in that manner concerning this period of a thousand years." Though he conceded earlier in the same chapter that his view was not universal by saying that he "and many who belong to the pure and pious faith, and are true Christians, think otherwise."

1. 1. Johannes Quasten, Patrology, Vol. 1 (Westminster, Maryland: Christian Classics, Inc.), 219. (14)
2. "Dialogue with Trypho (Chapters 31-47)". Newadvent.org. Retrieved 2014-01-24. (15)

So, our first question is easily answered the position held by early Church fathers was premillennialism, not originated by John Darby's Dispensational teaching. So, this gives strong evidence the early Church was influenced by men like the apostle John who taught his disciples a coming kingdom age called the Millennium. Also, long after 70 AD, and the destruction of the Temple in Jerusalem, the Church fathers were still looking for the Millennial kingdom. This makes Preterism disconnected from the Church fathers, who did not teach Preterist eschatology. In fact, in early Church history not one single Church Father can be found as a Preterist. No Christian teacher of the first two Church centuries taught the Preterist doctrine. Or the millennial kingdom was now, and the prophetic judgments of Book Revelation were already accomplished.

Now to the second question, did the Church fathers teach a time of trouble, a Tribulation, right before the Second Coming of Jesus Christ? This too, is not difficult to find as the Church Fathers connected the time of the earth's Tribulation with the Antichrist, the false Messiah.

Study of Church history shows that the church fathers closest to the apostles, also believed that the church would go through the Tribulation.

Didache (AD 100) "then shall appear the world-deceiver as Son of God, and shall do signs and wonders, and the earth shall be delivered into his hands, ...but they that endure in their faith shall be saved from under the curse itself. And then shall appear the signs of the truth; first, the sign of an out-spreading in heaven; then the sign of the sound of the trumpet; and the third, the resurrection of the dead; yet not of all, but as it is said: The Lord shall come and all His saints with Him. Then shall the world see the Lord coming upon the clouds of heaven." (Didache - Chapter 16) 16

Justin Martyr (AD 100-168) "O unreasoning men! understanding not what has been proved by all these passages, that two advents of Christ have been announced: the one, in which He is set forth as suffering, inglorious, dishonored, and crucified; but the other, in which He shall come from heaven with glory, when the man of apostasy, who speaks strange things against the Most High, shall venture to do unlawful deeds on the earth against us the Christians, who, having learned the true worship of God from the law, and the word which went forth from Jerusalem by means of the apostles of Jesus, have fled for safety to the God of Jacob and God of Israel;" (First Apology of Justin, Chapter 110) 17

Irenaeus (AD 140-202) "he who is to come shall slay three, and subject the remainder to his power, and that he shall be himself the eighth among them. And they shall lay Babylon waste, and burn her with fire, and shall give their kingdom to the beast, and put the Church to flight. After that they shall be destroyed by the coming of our Lord." (Against Heresies V, XXVI, 1) 18

Tertullian (AD 150-220) "that the city of fornication may receive from the ten kings its deserved doom, Revelation xviii and that the beast Antichrist with his false prophet may wage war on the Church of God: (On the Resurrection of the Flesh, Chapter 25) 19

Hippolytus (AD 160-240) "That refers to the one thousand two hundred and threescore days (the half of the week) during which the tyrant is to reign and persecute the Church, which flees from city to city, and seeks concealment in the wilderness among the mountains," (Treatise on Christ and Antichrist, 61) 20

Cyprian (AD 200-258) "For you ought to know and to believe, and hold it for certain, that the day of affliction has begun to hang over our heads, and the end of the world and the time of Antichrist to draw near, so that we must all stand prepared for the battle ... "The time

cometh, that whosoever killeth you will think that he doeth God service..." Nor let any one wonder that we are harassed with increasing afflictions, when the Lord before predicted that these things would happen in last times.
(Epistle of Cyprian LV, 1,2) 21

Nor let any one of you, beloved brethren, be so terrified by the fear of future persecution, or the coming of the threatening Antichrist, as not to be found armed for all things by the evangelical exhortations and precepts, and by the heavenly warnings. Antichrist is coming... but immediately the Lord follows to avenge our sufferings and our wounds. (Epistles of Cyprian, LIII, p.722) 22

Victorinus (AD 269-271) "He shall cause also that a golden image of Antichrist shall be placed in the temple at Jerusalem, and that the apostate angel should enter, and thence utter voices and oracles... The Lord, admonishing His churches concerning the last times and their dangers, ... three years and six months, in which with all his power the devil will avenge himself under Antichrist against the Church." (Commentary on the Apocalypse, 20:1-3) 23

Unless you want to twist the historical record of the early Church fathers, no Preterism was taught as doctrine. The position was Pre-Millennial, Pre-Tribulation, even after 70 AD.

The Third Question

Now what of the third question, did any of the Church Father's teach a rapture of the Church before the Second Coming of Jesus Christ?

Irenaeus (130 A.D. – 202 AD)

In the line of succession Irenaeus was a disciple of Polycarp, who was a disciple of the apostle John, who recorded the Book of Revelation. Irenaeus was very vigilant in his defense of the faith writing against Christian heretics. In his famous writing from Church history Irenaeus demonstrated He was premillennial and believed in a "catching up of the Church before the Great Tribulation." In Against Heresies 5:29 Irenaeus wrote: (24)

"And therefore, when in the end the Church shall be suddenly caught up from this, it is said, "There shall be tribulation such as has not been since the beginning, neither shall be." For this is the last contest of the righteous, in which, when they overcome, they are crowned with incorruption."

Cyprian (200 AD – 258 AD)

Cyprian was the bishop of Carthage, and a Christian martyr, being beheaded for his faith. In his treatise on the Christian faith Cyprian wrote:

"We who see that terrible things have begun, and know that still more terrible things are imminent, may regard it as the greatest advantage to depart from it as quickly as possible. Do you not give God thanks, do you not congratulate yourself, that by an early departure you are taken away, and delivered from the shipwrecks and disasters that are imminent? Let us greet the day which assigns each of us to his own home, which snatches us hence, and sets us free from the snares of the world and restores us to paradise and the kingdom."

Cyprian believed and taught other Christians that escape from the snares of this world, by early departure is possible. The deliverance would be by the Lord snatches us away, and then restores His paradise and kingdom. Unless you want to not take at face value Cyprian and allegorize his plain meaning, he teaches a catching away of faithful saints before the restoration of the kingdom. (25)

Ephraim the Syrian (306 AD – 373 AD)

Ephraim was a deacon in Syria, and later a bishop at Nisibis. In his treatise called; The Last Times; writhing about the end times, Ephraim wrote:

"See to it that this sentence be not fulfilled among you of the prophet who declares: "Woe to those who desire to see the day of the Lord!" For all the saints and elect of God are gathered, prior to the tribulation that is to come, and are taken to the Lord lest they see the confusion that is to overwhelm the world because of our sins. And so, brothers most dear to me, it is the eleventh hour, and the end of the world comes to the harvest, and angels, armed and prepared, hold sickles in their hands, awaiting the empire of the Lord.

And we think that the earth exists with blind infidelity, arriving at its downfall early. Commotions are brought forth, wars of diverse peoples and battles and incursions of the barbarians threaten, and our regions shall be desolated, and we neither become very much afraid of the report nor of the appearance, in order that we may at least do penance; because they hurl fear at us, and we do not wish to be changed, although we at least stand in need of penance for our actions!" (26)

Church Fathers Data: 27

https://www.logosapostolic.org/bible_study/RP355-9ChurchFathers.htm

Clearly Ephraim believes in a coming Great Tribulation, and the gathering of the Church before the Lord prior to that event. The text is clear and plain, easy to read with no implied meanings. Just a belief in gathering of the saints either prior to the Tribulation, or the gathering prior to the Great Tribulation.

These writings on their own do not prove the existence of a Pre-Tribulation Rapture. However, the weight of early Church doctrines and beliefs demonstrate John

Darby is not the author of Pre-Tribulation, or at least Great Tribulation gathering of the Church unto the Lord. As some early Church Fathers obviously held this position. Also, virtually almost all Christians of the first two centuries viewed the Kingdom to come as Pre-Millennial. Some of these men who were well know teachers in the first century Church, and some being directly connected to the apostle John, we should not discount their testimony.

Church father's do not make their doctrines automatically the true doctrine of the Bible, but like every other teacher should be examined under the light of Scriptures already written. So, we must question were Church fathers influenced by the original apostles like John. If so, is the Book of Revelation then during the first two centuries still looked upon as "future prophetic judgment?" We must answer the questions why these men were still looking for a coming Antichrist long after 70 AD. Also why did men who suffered greatly for the faith still look for a coming Great Tribulation? Also, many of these Church Father's wrote those beliefs after 70 AD, where Preterist teach all these things were accomplished then.

The conclusion must be John Darby did not originate the doctrine of future Tribulation; it has existed in the Church at least in the first two centuries. John Darby is not the originator of Pre-Tribulation, or Great Tribulation doctrine before the coming Millennial

Kingdom. It can only be said John Darby has a unique ordering of the Bible into "dispensations" which Darby connects to Pre-Tribulation Pre-Millennial end time eschatological doctrines. The uniqueness of Darby is in putting the Scriptures into distinct periods of time know as dispensations, not in Tribulation, Pre-Millennial doctrine, or our gathering unto the Lord in the sky know today as rapture.

The historical evidence on the Church Fathers positions is over whelming. John Darby was not the originator of Pre-Millennial doctrine, Pre-Tribulation doctrine or rapture doctrine. So as far as primitive beliefs in those three doctrinal positions attacking John Darby is like attacking the early Church fathers as their beliefs, are similar. Even though we can easily say John Darby is the Father of modern-day Dispensationalism, Darby by no means invented those three doctrinal positions. Now as a Preterist or Post Millennial you might attack the rapture based on John Darby as the originator, of Dispensationalism. However, Church history speaks clearly, Darby's uniqueness is Dispensational only. Even if you threw out the rest of Darby's Systematic methods, you still must deal with Church history and fathers to eliminate those three essential doctrines of early Church eschatology.

The same goes for Margret McDonald who many Christians who want to attack the rapture doctrine attribute Margret McDonald as the originator of the rapture doctrine.

"There have been a couple of attempts to locate a "source" for Darby's concept of the Rapture — the belief that a core of Christian believers who have died will be raised from the dead, and believers who are still alive and remain shall be "caught up together with them in the clouds to meet the Lord in the air" (1 Thess 4:17) in conjunction with the Second Coming of Jesus Christ. Some of these attempts imply that Darby's concepts originated from a "false" source. Samuel Prideaux Tregelles alleged that the concept was taken from one of the charismatic utterances in Edward Irving's church. Since Tregelles regarded the utterances as "pretending to be from God," his implication is that Darby's rapture is from a demonic source. Dave MacPherson built upon Tregelles's accusation, and claimed[5][6] that the source for Darby's rapture was from an Margaret MacDonald's 1830 vision of the end times.[7][8]

However, scholars think there are major obstacles that render these accusations untenable. It is clear that Darby regarded the 1830 charismatic manifestations as demonic and not of God.[4] Darby would not have borrowed an idea from a source that he clearly thought was demonic.[9] Also Darby had already written out his pretribulation rapture views in January 1827, 3 years prior to the 1830 events and any MacDonald utterance.[10] When MacDonald's utterance is read closely, her statements appear to present a post tribulations scenario ("being the fiery trial which is to try us" and "for the purging and purifying of the real members of the body of Jesus").[11][12] Confusion on this point was enhanced because while MacDonald's vision as first published in 1840 describes a post-tribulation view of the rapture, a version published in 1861 lacked two important passages that appear to present a post-tribulation view: "This is the fiery trial which is to try us. - It will be for the purging and purifying of the real members of the body of Jesus" and "The trial of the Church is from Antichrist. It is by being filled with the Spirit that we shall be kept".[8] For these and other reasons, dispensational scholars consider MacPherson's alleged connection to dispensationalism as untenable.[13]" (Wikipedia) 28

Why A Departure From 1st Century Rapture Expectation?

Why the change from the imminent return of the Lord and the catching up of the Church, to the gradual removal and rapture of the Church? Historian Kurt Aland also sees the early church imminent expectation of the Lord's return.

"Up until the middle of the second century, and even later, Christians did not live in and for the present, but they lived in and for the future; and this was in such a way that the future flowed into the present, that future and present became one—a future which obviously stood under the Lord's presence. It was the confident expectation of the first generations that the end of the world was not only near, but that it had already come. It was the definite conviction not only of Paul, but of all Christian of that time, that they themselves would experience the return of the Lord."

Curt Aland: History of Christianity: From the Beginnings to the Threshold of the Reformation, vol 1 Philadelphia Fortress Press; 1, 87 (29)

Aland sees the decline of a true imminence that began around a.d. 150.

As soon as the thought of a postponement of the Parousia was uttered once—and indeed not only incidentally, but thoroughly presented in an entire writing—it developed its own life and power. At first, people looked at it as only a brief postponement, as the Shepherd of Hermes clearly expresses. But soon, as the end of the world did not occur, it was conceived of as a longer and longer period, until finally—his is today's situation nothing but the thought of a postponement exists in people's consciousness. Hardly any longer is there the thought of the possibility of an imminent Parousia. Today we live with the presumption—I would almost say from the presumption—that this world is going to continue; it dominates our consciousness. Practically, we no longer speak about a postponement, but only seldom does the idea of the end of the world and the Lord's return for judgment even occur to us; rather, it is pushed aside as annoying and disturbing—in contrast to the times when faith was alive. It is very characteristic that in ages when the church flourishes, the expectation of the end revives—we think of Luther; we think of Pietism. If we judge our present time by its expectation of the future.

Aland, History of Christianity, I, 92. (30)

Chapter 5
Literal or Allegorical Interpretation

Darby's Dispensational Approach to Scriptures

"The original concept came when Darby considered the implications of Isaiah 32 for Israel. He saw that prophecy required a future fulfillment and realization of Israel's kingdom. The New Testament church was a separate program not related to that kingdom. Thus, arose a prophetic earthly kingdom program for Israel and a separate "Mystery" heavenly program for the church. In order to not conflate the two programs, the prophetic program had to be put on hold to allow for the church to come into existence. Then it is necessary for the church to be raptured away before prophecy can resume its earthly program for Israel.[23] Some critics have claimed that there was no Christian teaching of a rapture before Darby began preaching about it in the

1830s, but recent research has discovered many sources in the preceding 250 years showing a development of the concept.[24] In Darby's conception of dispensations, the Mosaic dispensation continues as a divine administration over earth up until the return of Christ. The church being a heavenly designated assembly does not have its own dispensation as per Scofield. Darby conceives of dispensations relating exclusively to the divine government of the earth and thus the church is not associated with any dispensations." (Wikipedia) 31

The Pre-Millennial, Pre-Tribulation and rapture position requires a literal approach to interpreting Scriptures. In comparison the Preterist doctrine of the Second Coming is based upon the allegorical, or symbolic spiritualizing of Scriptures not taking them for their literal face value. The difference is defined by what is called the historical-grammatical approach to Scriptures. Combined along with a belief in progressive revelation from the Old Testament to the New Testament. God has been progressively bringing greater light and understanding from the Old Testament ending with the canonization of the New Testament.

The historical grammatical principle based on historical, socio-political, geographical, cultural and linguistic grammatical context. Pre-Millennial Dispensationalists begin with progressive revelation in the Old Testament and read forward in a historical sense. Therefore, there is an emphasis on a gradually developed unity as seen in the entirety of Scripture. Dispensationalism emphasizes the original recipients to whom the different Biblical covenant promises were written. This has resulted in certain fundamental dispensational beliefs, such as a distinction between Israel and the Church.

Distinction between Israel and the Church

'Dispensationalists profess a definite distinction between Israel and the Church. For dispensationalists, Israel is an ethnic nation[6] consisting of Hebrews (Israelites), beginning with Abraham and continuing in existence to the present. The Church, on the other hand, consists of all saved individuals in this present dispensation—i.e., from the "birth of the Church" in Acts until the time of the Rapture.[7] According to Progressive Dispensationalism in contrast to the older forms, the distinction between Israel and the Church is not mutually exclusive, as there is a recognized overlap between the two.[8]:295 The overlap consists of Jewish Christians such as Peter and Paul, who are ethnically Jewish and also have faith in Jesus Christ.[9]Dispensationalists also believe that Israel as a nation will embrace Jesus as their messiah toward the end of the Tribulation, right before his second coming. The spectrum of teaching in Israel and the Church may be depicted as below." (Wikipedia) 32

Christians must consider who has final say, who has final authority. Authentic Christian faith must rest on the authority of Scriptures as their final authority. In Catholicism the authority rests with the Catholic Church over Scriptures and so tradition often replaces the Written Word of God. In the Protestant recovery of the authority of Scriptures the principles of "sola scripta," or in God's word alone was established. The Protestant Reformation was to recover the Scriptures as final authority over human philosophy and tradition. It is was in view of the original teachings of the Church fathers, and the recovery of doctrines by sola scripta, the doctrines of Pre-Millennialism, Pre-Tribulation, and Rapture were recovered. John Darby's historical-grammatical approach to God's dealings with humanity in different times, or dispensations, led Darby's Pre-Millennial Pre-Tribulation Rapture of the Church. Now with some of John Darby's other doctrines outside of eschatology we have "many concerns," as his soteriology is not in line with orthodox Protestant view of doctrine.

The Problem of Scriptural Inerrancy

The historical-grammatical approach to Bible interpretation stays with the literal interpretation of God's Written Word, as compared to the allegorical spiritualized method. As compared to the allegorical which has eliminated the Kingdom of heaven future at the Second Coming and Church rapture. Here is an example of how one post millennial teacher eliminates the literacy of Revelation chapter 20 teaching the millennial kingdom is not literal just symbolic.

An Excerpt from Bill Johnson:
"We have statements in Scripture concerning the beasts and the thousand years. For example, it says that the dragon will be bound with chains and cast into a bottomless pit for a thousand years. Now I do not want to take away your millennium . . . I just want to suggest that we might not know what we are talking about because there are only a couple of verses in the Bible on the subject!

Then Bill Johnson begins to ask questions of the audience. Z

Bill Johnson: The dragon, literal or figurative? Is it a real dragon?

Audience replies: Figurative.

Bill Johnson: The chains, literal or figurative? Is its actual chains?

Audience replies: Figurative.

Bill Johnson: The bottomless pit, literal or figurative?

Audience replies: Figurative.

Bill Johnson: The millennium, literal or figurative?

To this question, the audience replies only with stunned silence.

Bill then goes on to speak about how we have allowed our interpretation of the Millennium and other passages to cancel out our responsibility to demonstrate the Kingdom of God in the present—as if many of the Bible's promises are not for today. To that I (Welton) say, "That's a good word, Bill!"

One must question is Bill Johnson, right? Is Bill's Kingdom Now Theology rightly taught by making Revelation 20 spiritual instead of literal? How impressed is the Bethel Church audience with Bill teaching on no literal future Millennial Kingdom? With what authority has Johnson removed the age-old doctrine of the Millennial Kingdom? With the wave of his doctrinal wand, it is all over with the whole teaching of the Millennium which according to Bill Johnson is just a figure of speech.

Don Pirozok: Kingdom Come; A Biblical Response to Dominion Theology, Pilgrims Progress Publishing pgs. 52-53 (33)

Is Bill Johnson right to teach Revelation chapter 20 is just figurative and not the establishment of the Millennial Kingdom at the Second Coming of Jesus Christ. Bill Johnson is a Post Millennial Kingdom Now/Dominion Theology teacher who believes the

Church is the Kingdom of heaven on earth right now. As you can see the problem of a literal 1000-year rule is found in this 20th chapter of Revelation.

Kingdom Now Post Millennial or Kingdom Now Preterist teachers must deconstruct this chapter from it is literal historical- grammatical interpretation and place these events in history. The problem exists when you attempt to say everything is just a symbol or an allegory in this chapter. What happens when you come to the 5th and 6th verses in this 20th chapter? Are we to suppose the resurrection of the righteous dead are just a symbol or allegory too? You cannot teach some portions of this chapter are just allegory, while these two verses alone are literal? This would make for individual exegesis based upon private interpretations, and not a systematic Bible interpretive method. So, you could pick and choose what Scriptures you say are factual and literal, and then those you deem as symbolic.

So, either Bill's post Millennial approach of interpretation continues to verse five and six, where he must teach the resurrection of the righteous dead, is just a symbol too. Of course, this would make Bill Johnson a full-blown heretic, so in this teaching Bill stops before these verses.

While others who a Kingdom Now Preterist, teach the first resurrection must be assumed in this passage. In other words, the saints in this passage were raised from the dead into immortality at the resurrection of Jesus Christ and reign with the Lord from heaven. Other Preterist simply say there is no need for a future bodily return of Jesus Christ, or the bodily resurrection of the righteous dead. Of course, the denial of the resurrection is pure heresy, so Post Millennial denial of the literacy of the resurrection in chapter 20 puts them in a heretical position. To deny the literal coming Kingdom age of 1000 years (Millennium) in Revelation chapter 20 teachers must teach allegory method. Then deny the literal first resurrection making it spiritual or a spiritual new birth instead of a physical resurrection.

Revelation 20:1-6 (34)
1 And I saw an angel come
down from heaven, having the key of the bottomless
pit and a great chain in his hand.
2 And he laid hold on the dragon, that
old serpent, which is the
Devil, and Satan, and bound him a thousand years,
3 And cast him into the bottomless
pit, and shut him up, and set a seal upon him, that he
should deceive the nations no more, till the
thousand years should be
fulfilled: and after that he must be loosed a
little season.
4 And I saw thrones, and they
sat upon them, and judgment was given unto
them: and I saw the souls of them that were
beheaded for the witness of Jesus, and for the word of

God, and which had Not worshipped the
beast, neither his image, neither received his mark upon
their foreheads, Orin their hands and they
lived and reigned with Christ a thousand years.
5 But the rest of the dead lived not again until the
thousand years were finished. This is the first
resurrection.
6 Blessed and holy is he that hath part in the
first resurrection: on such the second death hath no
power, but they shall be priests of God and of
Christ, and shall reign with him a thousand years.

Let us face the facts historical-grammatical literal method of Bible exposition is at odds with the allegorical spiritualized methods of interpretation. In this case the two positions are diametrically opposed to each other, so they both cannot be right. So now Christians must face the facts one position is false, the other is likely true. Even though there are other eschatological positions other than Pre-Millennial, Post Millennial and Preterist. Christians need to examine teachers and doctrines in the light of the whole counsel of Scriptures.

For Christians who hold the Written Word of God as their final source of authority must stand upon the infallibility and inerrancy of the Bible. In this case, the Bible is always right and without error, so men will twist the Scriptures out of their proper historical-grammatically meaning to fit contemporary philosophies are become false teachers.

I have found those who hold the Preterist Kingdom Now/Dominion Theological eschatology must twist the Scriptures, Church history, and current reality to fit their Church/Kingdom worldwide take over. In this way Preterist do not stand behind the inerrancy of Scriptures. Are constantly guilty of deconstruction and reconstructing Scriptures according to Preterist philosophy.

In Christian eschatology the rapture refers to the controversial "predicted" end time event when all Christian believers—living and resurrected dead—will rise into the sky and join Christ for eternity.[1][2] Some Christians believe this event is predicted and described, using the Greek word "harpazo", "rapio" in Latin, meaning to snatch away or seize, in Paul's First Epistle to the Thessalonians in the Bible 1 Thessalonians 4:17. The term "rapture" has come especially to distinguish this event from the event of the "Second Coming" of Jesus Christ to Earth, as some think is predicted elsewhere in the Bible, in Second Thessalonians, Gospel of Matthew, First Corinthians and the Revelation.[3]
The term "rapture" is especially useful in discussing or disputing the exact timing or the scope of the event, particularly when asserting the "pre-tribulation" view that the rapture will occur before, not during, the

Second Coming, with or without an extended Tribulation period.[4] This is now the most common use of the term, especially among Christian theologians and fundamentalist Christians in the United States.[5] Other, older uses of "rapture" were simply as a term for any mystical union with God or for eternal life in Heaven with God.[6] Catholics believe that the "Rapture" as a gathering with Christ in Heaven will take place, though they do not generally use the word "Rapture" to refer to this event, sometime during the second coming of Christ.[7]
(Wikipedia) 35

Now that we have established the catching up of the Church into the clouds existed before John Nelson Darby and Margaret McDonald. Let us look at the connection to the Tribulation, technically those who hold to a coming Tribulation time at the end of this present evil age. Who place the Rapture either at the beginning of the Tribulation, or in the middle or at the end of the Tribulation? For the sake of discussion, we will define the length of the Tribulation period as seven years from beginning to end. Even though this 7-year time frame would be debated among many in the end time Tribulation camp. My purpose now is to address three positions of rapture: Pretribulation, Mid Tribulation and Post Tribulation. Depending on your end time views of the Tribulation if you are a futurist, not Preterist, or Post Millennial, you will hold to one of those three rapture positions.

Now the most popular by far readily adopted by modern day Evangelicals who follow the Scofield Bible is the Pre-Millennial position of Rapture.

"Pre-tribulation rapture theology was popularized extensively in the 1830s by John Nelson Darby and the Plymouth Brethren,[15] and further popularized in the United States in the early 20th century by the wide circulation of the Scofield Reference Bible.[16]" (Wikipedia) 36

What happened in the late 1700's to the late 1800's to recover the doctrine of the rapture and the Pre-Millennial kingdom? The Protestant Reformation recovered the position of justification by faith, instead of the Catholic salvation by the sacraments, and a Catholic priest. The Protestant Reformation is the practice of establishing the written Word of God, instead of the human philosophy and traditions of Catholicism. Church history demonstrates no first century Church fathers held the position the Church was the kingdom of heaven on earth. Neither was there any Church fathers which believed the Preterist position the Book of Revelation was 95% completed at the 70 AD Temple destruction in Jerusalem. However, all that changed with Catholicism when the Catholic Church was declared to be the Kingdom of Heaven on earth. So, the concept of the Millennial Kingdom and its connection with Israel and the Second Coming of Jesus Christ began to be recovered using the principles of the Protestant Reformation.

Why did Jesus say, "repent for the Kingdom of Heaven is at hand?" Was Jesus Christ announcing the starting of the Church, or something even a little more? The problem lies in connecting the Church with the Kingdom and making the Kingdom of heaven on earth the Church. For the first two hundred years of the Church, Christians who were mainly Jews looked for a literal coming rule of Jesus Christ. As the Son of David to sit as King from the Throne of David ruling over all the world. If the Church remained Jewish in nature, the Kingdom of heaven was always future based upon the Second Coming of Jesus Christ. That is why the Church of the first two hundred years, had an "any moment return" what we call immanency, as Christians were suffering horrible persecution, even martyrdom.

The suffering Jewish Church never thought the Kingdom of heaven was now. With Christians being beheaded and made to be entertainment with gladiators. Also put in with lions, placed in prison only looked to "escape the great Tribulation," by the imminent return of Jesus Christ. Jewish Christians were looking for a better resurrection, a better position in the coming Kingdom age. As the result would go to their deaths as martyrs not denying the Lord. This suffering Church was completely pre-Millennial, the Kingdom was "future," never associated with the Church. This fact of Church history is premillennial is such a reality, the early Church of Jews went by the title "Chiliast's" which means a 1000-year period. So, the Kingdom of Heaven was future, a millennial reign of Jesus Christ on earth for a literal 1000-year time frame. Of these facts any one can check and see, just look at Church historians, and the word Chiliasm.

Why wasn't their "one single Preterist among all the Church fathers of the first two hundred years. Not one Christian thought the Book of Revelation had been completed in 70 AD. The reason is obvious, getting your head cut off, or hanging on a Cross, or being set on fire as a human torch is not exactly the conditions described in the Millennial kingdom. So, for all most 400 years no Church Father taught the Preterist position. Then Origen, an Alexandrian from Egypt, suggested a "kingdom on earth," was too crude, to carnal for a holy God. So, Origen suggested Christians would experience the Kingdom in heaven. Origen was also the first heretic to teach, "all men would be saved out of Hell." (Universal Salvation) Now Origen is the champion of modern day Preterist as his primitive form of denying the Millennial kingdom, helps with their manmade doctrine. The Preterist Jesus Christ first returned in 70 AD, and the Kingdom of heaven is the Church.

Of Course, the Catholic Church is the originator of denying the coming future kingdom (millennial reign) and making the Church Kingdom now. Constantine declared the Catholic Church as the Kingdom of heaven of earth, and the Pope as God's head representative on earth. Now who was declared to be the ruler of the world and God's king on earth, Pope Constantine of course. So today in the Charismatic Preterist Church, Charismatics have the same spirit of the Catholic Church married to the worldly Kingdom. Christians are declared as "king priests," to take dominion over all the nations of the earth. So Preterist Christians have developed a theological system called Kingdom Now/Dominion theology to prove how the Kingdom of heaven is now through the Church, and now to take dominion over the earth.

Now are Christians still suffering for faith in Jesus Christ, and having their heads cut off, or put into prison? Of course, however Christians in the United States are the main propagator of the Kingdom Now Preterist heresy. Are these Preterist teaching Christians to be in prayer, and watching for the hastening of the Second Coming of Jesus Christ? The answer is no they are teaching watching for the Lords return in prayer. In fact, in their economy Jesus Christ cannot return until Charismatic Preterist make for a Christian Utopia world by purifying the 7 pillars of culture. In Charismatic Preterism you get to be a little god, a little pope, a king, a ruler with God's restored Dominion over the nations of the earth.

One final comment, if you were offered to be a king, or crucified what would you choose? Is it any wonder in a

Church age when Christians are married to the world, and think God's sign of blessing is prosperity? Charismatics teach all judgment is past also the absence of suffering the Cross. Instead, a Christian golden age making the kingdom of heaven already on earth?

Chapter 6
Does Jesus Christ Teach on Rapture?

After reviewing the historical ramifications of A Pre-Millennial, Pre-Tribulation, Rapture doctrinal belief in the early Church, and its recovery in the Protestant Reformation. Christians must then question does the Bible teach these doctrines? The most important question being did the head of the Church, Jesus Christ, teach the doctrine of the Rapture? Despite the protest of those who would deny the doctrine of Rapture, Jesus Christ did in fact teach a Rapture of Christians at the end of this age during the time of Tribulation. Here is the Scriptural proof of Christ's Tribulation Rapture teaching.

In Matthew chapter 24 Jesus gives a discourse on the Second Coming, the address is called the Olivet Discourse. Now Jesus Christ had just predicted the destruction of the Temple in Jerusalem, and His disciples wanted to know the timing of this event, and when they could see then end of this age, and the signs which would help them identify those times. Here are the 3 questions which the disciples wanted to know about the future: 1) When will these things be 2) What shall be the sign of your coming 3) And the end of the world (age)

Matthew 24:1-3 (37)
1 And Jesus went out, and departed from the temple: and his disciples came to him for to shew Him the buildings of the temple.
2 And Jesus said unto them, See ye not all these things? verily I say unto you, There shall not Be left here one stone upon another, that shall not be thrown down.
3 And as he sat upon the mount of Olives, the disciples came unto
him privately, saying, Tell us, when shall these things be? and what shall be the
sign of thy coming, and of the end of the world?

If you are a Preterist you put the entire chapter of Matthew 24 in the past at the destruction of the Temple in 70 AD. If you are post Millennial you put the Kingdom age at the first coming of Jesus Christ and His Resurrection, or during the first century Church. However, if your Pre-Millennial most of the Olivet Discourse is yet to be fulfilled at the end of this age at the Second Coming of Jesus Christ. If you are Pre-Millennial, only the first question; "when while these things be," are only partly answered, as the Jerusalem Temple was destroyed in 70 AD. Now the rest of this passage will address then the end of the age, and the signs surrounding His coming.

To truthful students of the Bible, the Second Coming is what is in view of much of the Matthew 24 passage. The disciples were attempting to find out when the Kingdom would be restored to Israel, and the prediction of the temple destruction created a question as how this could happen, if Jesus Christ were the predicted Son of David? For proof, the disciples were looking for the restoration of the Kingdom to Israel. Let us look at their question by saying their answer was to be realized after Jesus Christ was raised from the dead. "When they therefore were come together, they asked of him, saying,
" Lord, wilt thou at this Time restore again the kingdom to Israel?" (Acts 1:6) So we must not suppose the original disciples thought the Kingdom had already come, even after the resurrection of Jesus Christ were still looking for the Kingdom restoration to Israel. Christians must not put in a Post Millennial twist, or a Preterist Kingdom Now twist to Matthew chapter 24.

The truth is the original displaces were looking to Old Testament predictions of the coming Messiah, the Son of David who would restore the Kingdom to Israel. At the time of the Olivet Discourse, they were still looking for Jesus Christ to restore the Kingdom. The original disciples had no idea it would require two comings of Jesus Christ in order to restore the Kingdom to Israel. First Jesus Christ must die and then be raised, ascend to heaven to obtain the Kingdom, and then return with the kingdom and establish it on earth as the Millennial age.

Even though the disciples did not at this time know it would require two comings, Jesus Christ did know and taught accordingly. So, the Temple destruction in 70 AD is only a partial fulfillment of all which Jesus Christ predicted. The temple destruction would happen in 70 AD, and then another Jerusalem Temple would finalize Jesus prophecy at the Second Coming thousands of years later.

Jesus Christ helps the disciples locate the signs of His coming by identifying the time of the Antichrist and the Abomination of Desolation spoken by the prophet Daniel. Now Preterist attempt to say the Antichrist was Caesar Nero who committed suicide in 68 AD and was not even alive in the 70 AD Roman invasion. Preterist should realize Nero could never fulfill the literal events predicted by Scriptures as the false Messiah. So, Nero, along with many other evil and wicked rulers who opposed the Jews and slaughtered them with military action were just "forerunners in history," shadowing the coming and literal Antichrist at the end of the age. Once Jesus Christ locates the literal Antichrist at the end of the age, He is addressing the signs of His coming, and what will transpire to end the world (age).
Let us look at some of the signs which precede His coming.
1) The gospel of the Kingdom to be preached all over the world, then comes the end. (Matthew 24:14)

2) Abomination of Desolation by the Antichrist spoken by the prophet Daniel. (Matthew 24:15)
3) Jews who refuse to bow to Antichrist must flee to the wilderness to escape his persecution. (Matthew 24:16-20) Notice how Jesus teaches them to pray their flight would not be on the Sabbath (typical for Jews, not Gentiles, or the Church)
4) The Great Tribulation in which God pours out His wrath all over the world and upon the Kingdom of the Antichrist. These judgments will never again happen as nothing since the creation equals their devastation. (Matthew 24:21-22)
5) False Christ's and Prophets arise to attempt to deceive the elect with lying signs and wonders. (Matthew 24:23-24)
6) The Lord's Coming for the Jews will be like the lightening in the sky shining from east to west. A physical visible appearing where every eye shall behold Him. Jesus Christ will not appear on earth first, as the false Christ's and false prophets will present first. (Matthew 24:23-28)
7) After the first part of the Tribulation, the final judgments of God will darken the sun, and moon, and the stars will fall as God brings catastrophic judgments against the heavens. (Matthew 24:29)
8) Now as the final Trumpet sounds the Lord gathers the grapes of wrath in harvest, but

> before then the wheat is gathered and garnered in heaven. (Matthew 24:30-31)

Jesus Christ makes for one of the great signs before His coming "the Rapture." In Matthew chapter 24 verses twenty-seven through thirty-one describe the sign of His coming, the Rapture of the Church. Why would God provide a sign of His coming, instead of just the bursting forth of God out of heaven where every eye shall behold Him? The sign of Christ's coming suggest the process of the Second Coming takes place over time, at least three- and one-half years, and many teach the Tribulation is seven years in length. The Rapture of the Church both the dead and the living is a sign to the elect Jews and the Gentile world the final judgments of God are approaching and the end of this age.

How can the Rapture be explained as part of the process of the Second Coming? The coming of the Son of Man, Jesus Christ, is a descent out of heaven with a shout of the arch angel, and the trumpet of God. It is the call to the gathering of the Church up from the earth into the clouds of the sky. In the rapture or gathering of the saints is the descent of the Lord Jesus Christ from heaven to the atmosphere of the earth, but not the full descent upon the earth. The rapture is described as the saints being gathered with the Lord not on earth instead into the heavens, the clouds of the sky.

We must separate the Greek words used for coming. Regarding the catching up of the Church into the sky the word used for coming is "Parousia." In English, the word has been translated as "coming," but in the Greek it is translated into the word "presence." First the Lord will descend from His throne with the Glory of His presence, a cloud of His presence into the earth's atmosphere. The sign of the hidden presence of the Lord is related by Scriptures as "thief coming in the night," to steal away valuable articles. In this case those valuable articles are the watching prayerful saints who are looking for His coming.

The second word translated "coming," in connection to the Second Coming of the Lord is the Greek word; "epiphaniea." First the decent of the actual presence of the Lord into the heavens concealed by the clouds of His glory, the Secret appearing of the Lord for the rapture of the Church. Then the visible breaking forth of the presence of Jesus Christ several years later as every eye shall behold Him. Notice the distinction between the two words translated in English as coming:
"It is a matter of great consequence to distinguish between the Parousia or actual presence of Christ in the atmospheric heavens at the first stage of His coming, and the epiphaneia or visible manifestation of that presence to the world years later at its second stage. A significant distinction is apparently observed in Scripture in the use of these terms - the word Parousia occurring twenty-four times, and the expression epiphaneia six times in the

New Testament. The difference between these two words may thus be explained. The moon may sometimes have risen on a cloudy night above the horizon for five hours, and yet not be visible because of interposing dark clouds which shut it out from our view; nevertheless there is during those five hours an actual (although invisible) presence or Parousia of the moon in the ethereal heavens: and when at last the intervening clouds are suddenly withdrawn, the lunar orb becomes at once visible to every upturned eye; this is the epiphaneia, or open manifestation of its previous Parousia or presence.

Similarly, there will be the Parousia or bodily Presence of the Lord Jesus in the ethereal heavens when He descends from heaven into the air, before the epiphaneia, or open manifestation of that Parousia to the world at large, by the withdrawal of the intervening clouds of concealment which will have intermediately shrouded Him from the observation of mortal man.

 Various predictions intimate that watchful Christians shall be kept out of and escape the final direful season of Tribulation, and that they may expect redemption even when it begins to come to pass. "Because thou hast kept the word of My patience (that is, the injunction patiently to wait for My Coming), I also will keep thee from the hour of temptation, which shall come upon all the world, to try them that dwell upon the earth." "Watch ye therefore and pray always that ye may be

accounted worthy to escape all these things that shall come to pass, and to stand before the Son of man." "When these things BEGIN to come to pass, then look up..."
MichaelBaxter:
http://www.themillennialkingdom.org.uk/Parousia and Epiphany.htm (38)

Chapter 7
The Sign of Christ's Presence

Let us take a closer at the secretive presence of Christ hidden from the world for the purpose of gathering the saints into the sky. The decent of the Lord from the Throne at the right hand into the mid heavens is the sign of His presence. Not to be confused with the actual coming of the Lord with the armies of heaven. The Scriptures distinguish between the two comings of Jesus Christ, one "coming for" the saints in rapture, the other "coming with" the saints as the Lord of Hosts, the army of God. A picture of God obscured by clouds of glory was experienced by the nation of Israel at Mount Sinai. Jesus Christ descends from the Throne where His descent is arrested in the mid heavens, into the sky of the earth, where the clouds of His glory conceal His presence.

The descent of the Lord into the mid heavens, or the clouds of the sky is the sign of His presence. It also signals to the saints the time of their great escape, and to the world, the sign of God's coming wrath. So, Christians need to distinguish by Scriptures the sign of His presence as connected with the catching up of the Church into Rapture. Let us look at the significance of the Presence of the Lord as connected to the Rapture. In the picture given at Mount Sinai God spoke out of the fire of His clouds of glory, Israel heard His voice but saw no form. (Deuteronomy 4:12&15)

Now what are we to expect in the catching up of the saints with the clouded glory and secret presence of the Lord? Are we to expect the whole world to see the rapture, like what Tim Lahaye has recorded in his books and movies? What has made the Left Behind movies popular is the sensationalizing of the Rapture. As often in Hollywood Biblical portraits of Scriptural events the truth is not often fully displayed. Tim Lahaye did a nice job for Hollywood to display the truth of a secret rapture, with one taken and the other left behind. However, many questions arise on how the glorification of the saints taken in rapture could be so hidden from the understanding of the world? As after the Rapture event the world is not any more alarmed, instead responds with the message of peace and safety. The rapture of the saints signals the time of God's wrath is at hand, but no apparent increased alarm comes from the response of the world.

1 Thessalonians 5:2-3 (39)
2 For yourselves know perfectly that the day of the Lord so cometh as a thief in the night.

3 For when for when they shall say peace and safety then sudden destruction cometh upon them, as travail upon a woman with child; and they shall not escape.

I would suggest Tim Lahaye's version of the whole world effected by the Rapture is fictitious, instead is more of a sign for the Church. Here are some facts we should consider about the secretive thief like appearing of the Lord for the rapture of the ready saints. Some Bible facts which must be addressed about rapture:

1) The Sign Is for the Church: The main purpose is to remove the saints from harm's way, and to prepare them for the Judgment Seat of Christ.

2) The World Responds with Peace and Safety: The effect upon the world is minimal, they respond by saying peace and safety.

3) The Saints Are Not Seen Ascending: This could be the result of the quickness of the saint's ascent into the sky. Or the small number of Christians which are originally taken.

4) Several Years Transpire Before the Lord Returns with the Saints: The saints which qualify for the rapture do not ascend, then immediately descend with the Lord to earth. Instead, several years will transpire between the Lord's appearing and

rapture, and then every eye beholding Him bursting forth from the clouds.

5) Accounts with the Saints Are Settled at Judgment Seat: The time of the saint's judgment is after the Rapture and before the Second Coming. The saints must appear at the Judgment Seat of Christ in the heavens to receive rewards and responsibility, or their loss.

6) The World Is Completely Ignorant of the Events Which Glorify the Saints: All the events of the saint's judgment, and glorification, are hidden from the view of the world. So as the Antichrist is assembling his Bride and army on earth so does the Lord glorify His bride and army in Heaven.

Jesus Christ Teaches His Thief in the Night Rapture

Jesus Christ expounds on His secret rapture presence, by describing His appearing as a "thief in the night." Jesus makes promise the last generation before the Second Coming of the Lord will see all these things. Heaven and earth shall pass away, but His prophetic predictions of the last days will not fail.
(Matthew 24:35)

But of the day and hour of His secret presence, the rapture of the Church, and the Second Coming, knows no man not even the angels of heaven, but only God the Father. Which eliminates the Preterist View of 70 AD, and those who attempt to date set the Coming of the Lord. However, the Lord gives us additional information regarding the time of the rapture.

"But as the days of Noe were, so shall also the coming of the Son of man be." (Matthew 24:37) Now the spiritual climate of the world before the Rapture is described by Jesus Christ as like the time before Noah entered the Ark and the flood came and took them all away.

"For as in the days that were before the flood they were eating and drinking, marrying and giving in marriage, until the day that Noe entered into the ark, and knew not until the flood came, and took them all away; so shall also the coming of the Son of man be." (Matthew 24:38-39)

As much as Kingdom Now/Dominion Theology attempt to teach the worldwide takeover of the Church, end time Scriptures point to a completely different scenario. The Days of Noah are recorded in Genesis chapter six which teaches wickedness and violence which permeated the whole earth right before the Great Flood.

Three factors are given about the time of the Lord's appearing 1) thief in the night secret presence 2)

Conditions as in the days of Noah 3) One taken and one left behind in rapture.

Are There Left Behind Christians

40 Then shall two be in the field; the one shall be taken, and the other left.
41 Two women shall be grinding at the mill; the one shall be taken, and the other left.
(Matthew 24:40-41) 40

From these Scriptures no one can say at the thief like coming of the Lord all are taken. Clearly, one is taken, and one is left behind. The picture is one who comes in the darkness of the night (Tribulation) and enters the house as a thief to steal valuable goods. Now the thief can discern between valuable treasures and those which are not authentic riches, so He takes the valuable treasure and leaves the rest behind. Now in this case the valuable treasure is taken, while the others are left. So, a question must be asked does the Lord discriminate between Christians in Rapture, as valuable and less valuable? Of course, all Christians are of great value to Jesus Christ in terms of salvation, but not all Christians have the same level of dedication or consecration. So, are the taken Christians then valuable as the result of consecration and godly living in a time when other Christians are caught up with the things of the world?

Now many Christians attempt to argue those left behind are not Christians, or just the Jewish elect are left behind, while all Christians are taken. However, the following Scriptures clearly identify both the taken and the left behind were all Christians. The Pre-Tribulation Rapture is not to remove any except the watchful praying Church.

42 Watch therefore: for ye
know not what hour your Lord doth come.
43 But know this, that if the goodman of the house had known in what watch the thief would come, he would have watched, and would not have
suffered his house to be broken up.
44 Therefore be ye also ready: for in such an hour as ye think not the Son of man cometh. (Matthew 24:42-44) (41)

The breakdown of these Scriptures are as follows: 1) Watching saints are looking for the coming rapture. 2) The hour of the Rapture in not known by anyone in the Church prior to the Lord's presence (coming). If the goodman would have known when the thief would come, he would have watched. 3) Suffering your house to be broken into is compared to slumbering Christians not found prepared at the Presence of the Rapture. 4) Therefor be ready for you will not be prepared if you are not looking for His coming.

The fact the one taken, and one left is Christian is defined by the words; "your Lord does come." The rest of these passages confirm the Lord of that servant taken or left speaks only of Christians. Who then is the faithful and wise Christian, is the same one taken as the valuable treasure by the thief in the night (rapture)? The faithful servant of Jesus Christ can only be a born-again Christian, as the world is a natural enemy to God, and the Jews have rejected Jesus Christ as their Messiah.

The fact the Lord rewards the faithful and wise servant taken in rapture proves all taken are Christians. Will the Lord reward unbelievers at His coming making them rulers over His household? Of course not, those whose names which are not written in the Book of Life are judged at the Great White Throne, not taken and rewarded in rapture. Blessed is the servant of the Lord the faithful watching Christian who is the Lord finds prepared at His coming. This one will be taken in rapture while the unfaithful Christian who did not look or prepare himself for the presence of the Lord is left behind.

45 Who then is a
faithful and wise servant, whom his lord hath made ruler over his household, or give them meat in due season?
46 Blessed is that servant, whom his lord when he cometh shall find so doing.

47 Verily I say unto you, That he shall
make him ruler over all his goods.
(Matthew24:45-47) 42

However, does the Lord ever call Christian servants evil? What does the evil servant say in his heart, "My Lord delays His coming?" Does the unbeliever identify Jesus Christ as His Lord, or even give their lives to serve the Lord? Absolutely not, those who are being identified by the Lord are wicked and unprofitable servants who have fallen to the sins of the world. "And shall begin to smite his fellow servants (Christians) and to eat (gluttony) and drink (surfeiting, party life) with the drunken." The Lord of that servant when he looks not, means this Christian is worldly in sin and left behind at the rapture. In the time the Lord catches up the faithful Pre-Tribulation saints, the wicked servant is caught in the cares of this world and is not prepared for His coming. Not only is the wicked servant not taken, at the Judgment Seat of Christ when he eventually does appear, he is appointed to the portion of the hypocrites (place for unfaithful Christians). There shall be weeping and gnashing of teeth.

48 But and if that evil servant shall
say in his heart, My lord delayeth his coming;
49 And shall begin to smite his fellow servants, and to
eat and drink with the drunken;

50 The lord of that servant shall come in a day when he looketh not for him, and in an hour that He is not aware of,
51 And shall
cut him asunder, and appoint him his portion with the hypocrites: there shall be weeping and gnashing of teeth.
(Matthew 24:48-51) 43

In the Rapture, Scriptures teach the Church's escape is with the Lord into the clouds into the air. While at the same time the Jewish elect must escape by fleeing into the wilderness which is outside Jerusalem. So, the sealed elect Jews are not taken in rapture, as no unbelievers will appear before the Judgment Seat of Christ. Only the Church, all the saints who have names written in the Book of Life appear at the Judgment Seat. So, the left behind in the rapture passages cannot be anyone except Christians, born again believers in Jesus Christ.

An excerpt by Watchman Nee:

"In order to understand Matthew 24 and 25, it is essential to have a clear knowledge of the subject of rapture. For it is one of the most important matters in this last hour. Unfortunately, it is greatly misunderstood by many.

There are different views on rapture among believers. Some say (1) that the whole body of the saved will be raptured before the Great Tribulation; others believe (2) that the whole body of the saved must go through the Great Tribulation before they are raptured; while still others feel (3) that a part of the saved will be raptured before the Great Tribulation and a part of them will be raptured after the Great Tribulation. There are mainly these three schools of interpretation on the subject; yet merely because one of them is different from the other does not give you any warrant to denounce the different view as heresy. It is wrong to withhold fellowship simply for this reason.

Well-known believers are found in all three schools. Of the first school mentioned, names can be cited such as J. N. Darby, William Kelly (C. H. Spurgeon once said that Kelly's brain was as large as the universe), R. A. Torrey (who later changed to a post-tribulation rapture view), Phillips Brooks, James Gray, Arno C. Gaebelein, J. A. Seiss, C. I. Scofield, and so forth.

Of the second school, there could be listed such names as George Muller (who first believed in pre-tribulation rapture), A. J. Gordon of Boston, A. B. Simpson, W. J. Erdman, W. G. Moorehead, Henry Frost of Canada, James Wright, Benjamin Newton, and so on.

And as to the third school, we have names such as Hudson Taylor, Robert Chapman, Robert Govett

(Spurgeon praised his writings as having light a century ahead of his time and as being full of gold), G. H. Pember, D. M. Panton (the "prince of prophecy") and others.

None of the three schools can completely ignore the others, yet only one is correct. Let us therefore examine them with fairness, having the attitude of a judge and not that of a lawyer."
Watchman Nee:"The King and the Kingdom", p. 271 CFP, Co. 1978) 44

Chapter 8
First Fruits and Harvest

The most popular rapture position among Protestant Evangelicals is the Pre-Tribulation rapture. The basic concept is the whole Church, which is saved by faith in Jesus Christ, is then removed at the beginning of Tribulation time. The thought is the Cross has given salvation both from sin, hell, the coming wrath of God, and so the entire Church of the redeemed is removed at this time. In this way the rapture is provided as part of the gift of grace and has nothing to do with the Christian's dedication or consecration after coming to saving faith.

The completely opposite position is taught by Post Tribulation Christian teachers, who insist the rapture of the Church manifests only after the Tribulation time frame is complete. Most in the modern Church place the Tribulation as the last seven years of this present age, and are the culmination of the Church age, before the Millennial Kingdom of Heaven on earth. In this way rapture is also considered a gift of grace included in the salvation of the Cross. No amount of consecration or dedication can rapture the Church, instead all Christians must fully go through the trial of Tribulation together.

Another position is offered which is not Pre-Tribulation rapture, or Post Tribulation rapture, instead all Christians will be removed halfway into the Tribulation (31/2 years). This is also considered a gift of grace which no amount of dedication or consecration by Christians can effect a change. None by their consecration can improve their rapture position into Pre-Tribulation or lose it in a Post Tribulation rapture. So, all three of these positions are not based upon any Christian ability or effort.

Multiple Raptures and 1st Resurrection

A fourth position of rapture exists, but is not very well know, and not popular even when being taught. It consists of a "selective rapture," instead of all Christians taken in a single rapture event, Christians are not removed together in one rapture event. Instead of one rapture at the beginning, or their middle, or the end, there are multiple raptures and removals. Now selective rapture has the element of human reward for dedication and faithfulness after coming to saving faith.

In this position all Christians will be raptured, but every man, woman, and child taken according to their state of preparedness. In the selective rapture the concept of sanctification is included, and Christians who are more consecrated, by prayer, watchfulness and holy living can "improve their rapture position."

The whole selective rapture position is based upon Christians being viewed as grain for harvest. Some of the grain ripens before the rest of the crop it is harvested earlier, being identified as the "first fruits harvest." So consecrated holy Christians who by reason of watchful prayer have made themselves ready to be taken before others are then considered the valuable first fruits of harvest. While most of the crop (wheat grain) is left in the Tribulation sun, the trials of heat and pressure to bring them into harvest maturity. So, after the first Fruits are taken in a Pretribulation rapture, most Christians are left behind facing the Tribulation. Then about mid-way in the Tribulation, during the early stages of the Antichrist the bulk of Christians are raptured out before the wrath of God is poured out in the seven vial judgments. This might be considered a Mid Tribulation rapture and would include most Christians which were first left behind. This position is defined by the Great Multitude in heaven in Revelation chapter seven.

Now after the "Great Multitude is taken into heaven," only a small portion of the harvest remains, which is called the gleanings. Some Christians are obviously present during the time of the Antichrist and must suffer terrible persecution with many being martyred. Now the final taking of the saints occurs after the Great Tribulation. Which occurs at the end of the whole 7 seven years after the first fruits harvest, and 3 ½ years after the Mid Tribulation harvest. The final catching up of this small portion of Great Tribulation saints would be considered a Post Tribulation Rapture.
The selective rapture is often identified by it is first fruits and Harvest multiple raptures teachings. If Christians were to think about the debate between Pre-Tribulation, Mid Tribulation, and Post Tribulation rapture, selective rapture might be a reasonable explanation. The question being can all three rapture positions be identified by Scriptures and is the explanation why some defend one rapture position against the others? The only way we can reasonably answer this question is to present the Scriptural evidence for its reality. Otherwise, selective rapture is a theory with no real basis in the authority of Scriptures. So, let us investigate the evidence of a first fruits and harvest selective rapture(s)?

The apostle Paul can help us in this matter by teaching there is an order to the resurrection. First, Christians must understand there are two resurrections the first resurrection happens after the Tribulation and at the

Second Coming of the Lord. The second resurrection is one thousand years later, after the millennial kingdom of heaven on earth. So, we must understand only the saints can qualify for the first Resurrection which happens at the Judgment Seat of Christ in Heaven and not before the saints are taken by rapture. No unbeliever, no unsaved person can appear at the Judgment Seat of Christ, so the first Resurrection is for the righteous only, and the wicked do not appear.

1 Corinthians 15:22-27 (45)
22 For as in Adam all die, even so in Christ shall all be made alive.
23 But every man in his own order: Christ The first fruits; afterward they that are Christ's at his coming.
24 Then cometh the end, when he shall have delivered up the kingdom to God, even the Father; when he shall have put down all rule and all authority and power.
25 For he must reign, till he hath
put all enemies under his feet.
26 The last enemy that shall be destroyed is death.
27 For he hath put all things under his feet. But when he saith all things are put under him, it is manifest that he is excepted which did put all things under him.

Notice the first resurrection has an order, with Jesus Christ being the first, then those of like nature first fruits, followed by those who are Christ's at His appearing or "Parousia." So, the first fruits rapture is before the Lord descends into the mid heavens of the earth in His secret appearing. Now when the Lord does appear the Great Multitude of the Harvest which now is in the heat and fire of Tribulation have washed their garments from being stained by the world and is ready for harvest. Some however, must go through the entire Tribulation, and some are saved during the time of the Antichrist will then be the last to be taken in the final rapture. Let us compare order of the rapture/resurrection to the events of the Book of Revelation.

In Revelation chapter four a door opens in heaven through which the apostle John is invited to enter and being part of the first fruits Pre-Tribulation rapture. A small portion of saints given Pre-Tribulation rapture are redeemed from the earth are given heavenly thrones and positions. The first fruits harvest is the most rewarded of the saints, in both coming from the living Church and those saints who died in faith, like Abraham, Isaac and Jacob. To them is given authority and privilege to occupy seats next to the Lord in governance of the Kingdom age.

Revelation 5:9-14 (46)
9 And they sung a new song, saying, Thou art worthy to take the book, and to open the seals thereof: for thou wast slain, and hast redeemed us to
God by thy blood out of every kindred, and tongues, and people, and nation;
10 And hast made us unto

our God kings and priests: and we shall reign on the earth.
11 And I beheld, and I heard the voice of
many angels round about the throne and the
beasts and the elders: and the number of them was ten thousand times ten thousand, and thousands of thousands;
12 Saying with a loud voice, Worthy is the Lamb that was slain to
recieve power, and riches, andwisdom, and strength, and honour, and glory, and blessing.
13 And every creature which is in heaven, and on the earth, and under the earth, and such as are in the sea, and all that are in them, heard
I saying, Blessing, and honour, and glory, and power, be unto him that sitteth upon the throne, and unto the Lamb for ever and ever.
14 And the four beasts said, Amen. And the
four and twenty elders fell down and worshipped him that liveth for ever and ever.

Notice the twenty-four elders now sing a song of redemption after the first fruits rapture. Which suggests a heavenly exchange has happened where glorified saints now occupy thrones of government in heaven, which were formerly held by universal elders (likely angels). Now the glorified saints which have qualified in selective rapture are rewarded with new positions as kings/priests in the unfolding of the kingdom of heaven age on earth. As the first fruits rapture occurs before the Lord leaves His throne in Heaven to descend in the mid heavens (sky) of the earth, no secret presence of the Lord is indicated. Only a departure of a small portion of ripened saints which were alive on earth, and a portion of saints who were awaiting their resurrection which have qualified as the first fruits of Rapture/Resurrection.

Now the facts those of Revelation chapters five are redeemed glorified men are as follows:
1) They sang a new sung of redemption indicating Jesus Christ was slain by the Cross, and by His blood they were redeemed. No angel will ever be experienced redemption through the Cross, as no fallen angel will ever be offered redemption from their rebellion.
2) You have made us kings/priests and we shall reign, not in heaven but on earth, indicating the coming establishment of the millennial kingdom. Only the resurrected glorified saints are given thrones and crowns to rule in their glorified bodies during the Millennial Kingdom.
3) Now the rest of the angels join in the procession around the throne of worshiping Jesus Christ for redeeming these men from out of the earth, and Christ's right of rule after going through the Cross to the Throne, and now receiving the Kingdom from the Father (God)
4) The glorified saints are recorded as leading the worship procession and are clearly identified the

Church of the "first born sons" in heaven, the Church of the redeemed. The first fruits harvest, the first in rapture, and glorification, before the second rapture, which will only manifest after many seals of God's judgment are released.
5) This is part of the glorified army of saints which Jude writes about Enoch saying will come with the Lord as ten thousands of His glorified saints, to defeat the Antichrist.

The first fruits rapture is also identified in other portions of the Book of Revelation. In chapter fourteen the apostle John is given another view of the first fruits rapture which are presented as the chaste virgins of Christ.

Revelation 14:1-5 (47)
1 And I looked, and, lo, a Lamb stood on the mount Sion, and with him an hundred forty and fourthousand, having his Father's name written in their foreheads.
2 And I heard a voice from heaven, as the voice of many waters, and as the voice of a great thunder: and I heard the voice of harpers harping with their harps:
3 And they sung as it were a new song before the throne, and before the four beasts, and the elders: and no man could learn that song but the one hundred and forty and four thousand, which were redeemed from the earth.
4 These are they

which were not defiled with women; for they
are virgins. These are they which follow the
Lamb whithersoever he goeth. These were
redeemed from among men, being the first
fruits God and to the Lamb.
5 And in their mouth was found no guile: for they
are without fault before the throne of God.

Notice those who appear before God are accounted as standing on Mount Zion the place of God's throne in heaven. Their number is small compared to the whole of the Church as only 144,000 are selected to come and stand before God as first fruits, chaste virgins of Jesus Christ. Once again, an order to the resurrection is being emphasized where some of the Church is included by means of qualification while other larger portions of the saints are not so numbered and are excluded.

Can Holiness Give You A Better Resurrection

Sometimes modern Christianity misses out on the significance of how holy living now can affect your future resurrection. A great amount of New Testament teaching is devoted to instruction on a better resurrection at the Second Coming of Jesus Christ. Some of more obvious passages are the parables of the Talents, Pounds, and 10 Virgins. Each of these parables were taught by Jesus Christ and demonstrate rewards or loss of rewards, "after the return of Jesus Christ." Living a faithful devoted life of faith, prayer, and holy consecration makes for a better resurrection. The significance being some Christians sell out their "birth right," the right to rule and reign with Jesus Christ in the next age, for the "love of this world." Few are they who seek first the kingdom and lay up their treasures in heaven where at the Coming of Jesus Christ their rewards of consecration will be realized.

The modern Church tempts you towards worldly riches, personal success, and personal kingdom building. Instead, Jesus Christ teaches do not pursue riches, or living for the things of this world, put first Jesus Christ, and seek Godly holy living then you can be rewarded with Kingdom of heaven rewards in the next age. To seek first the Kingdom of heaven "does not mean bringing heaven to earth" as taught by the 7 Mountain gospel. Instead, it means picking up the Cross in self-denial and trusting in the coming Kingdom of Heaven on earth when Jesus Christ brings it upon His return.

Now the temptation to put the world's richest before Jesus Christ, and put the "kingdom in this age," stops Christians looking for a future resurrection and reward. Many simply are not seeking first the Kingdom at the resurrection, and instead are building their own kingdoms of self-seeking desires and calling it God. It takes faith in God to pick up the Cross looking for a future Kingdom, and not putting your heart and treasures in this world.

Enoch was a man who walked with God and the Lord took Him before Enoch saw death. Enoch had this testimony before the Lord "raptured him alive," Enoch pleased God. Despite modern day Church unbelief, the rapture of men alive into the heavens is a sign of God's pleasure and blessing. In this case rapture before death is treated as a reward for faithful holy living. The same could be said of Elijah the prophet who was raptured alive, as Elijah withstood the prevailing apostasy of his day.

Hebrews 11:5 (48)
5 By faith Enoch was translated that he
should not see death; and was not found, because God had translated him: for before his translation he had this testimony, that he pleased God.

Now that God rewards the faithful at His coming is seen in the martyrs of Revelation chapter 20. Those Christians refused to take the Mark of the Beast and worship the Antichrist during the time of the Great Tribulation. In reward are given the first resurrection, are made immortal men, and given thrones to sit and rule as kings and priests during the Millennial Kingdom age. However, the rest of the dead who were not faithful, or who were not holy lived not again until one thousand years which is the first resurrection. Blessed and holy is he who has part in the first resurrection.

We have seen many Scriptures which point to God selecting out the faithful from the unfaithful. The parables of the Talents, Pounds, 10 virgins all point to a selection of some and a shutting out of the rest. We can close our eyes to the facts of Scripture, men have been raptured as rewards for Godly holy living, and others not qualifying for translation out of Tribulation then suffer through it. The Scriptures prove the saints can obtain a better resurrection by Godly living. Can a Christian obtain a better resurrection, a better translation, before the Second Coming of Jesus Christ? Will some Christians be left behind not being rewarded instead of being faithful as Enoch was? Is this not the point of a selective rapture and a better resurrection?

The Great Multitude in Heaven

Compared to the First Fruits Pre-Tribulation Rapture the gathering of the Great Multitude in Heaven constitutes the main body of harvest. The Great Multitude is gathered at the opening of the sixth seal during the time of the Great Tribulation. Two events are recoded in the seventh chapter which demonstrate the two different people groups which are protected by the Lord during the Great Tribulation. The first group is the 144,000 elect Jews which are sealed by the Lord for protection, and their escape is by flight into the wilderness. The second group are Christians who have come to faith in Jesus Christ and are now ripened for harvest after several years of end time Tribulation. The Great Harvest of Christians are caught up in Rapture before the Throne of God out of the Great Tribulation.

Revelation 7:9-17 (49)
9 After this I beheld, and, lo, a great multitude, which no man could number, of all nations, andkindreds, and people, and tongues, stood before the throne, and before the Lamb, clothed with white robes, and palms in their hands;
10 And cried with a loud voice, saying, Salvation to our God which sitteth upon the throne, and unto the Lamb.
11 And all the angels stood round about the throne, and about the elders and the four beasts, and fell before the
Throne on their faces, and worshipped God,
12 Saying, Amen: Blessing, and glory, and wisdom, and thanksgiving, and honour, and power, andmight, be unto our God for ever and ever. Amen.
13 And one of the elders answered, saying unto me, What are these which are arrayed In white robes? and whence came they?
14 And I said unto him, Sir, thou knowest. And he said to me, These are they which came out of great tribulation, and have
washed their robes, and made them white in the blood of the Lamb.
15 Therefore are they before the throne of God, and serve him day and night in his temple: and he that sitteth on the throne shall dwell among them.

16 They shall
hunger no more, neither thirst any more; neither shall
the sun light on them, nor any heat.
17 For the Lamb which is in the midst of the throne shall
feed them, and shall lead them unto living fountain of
waters: and God shall wipe
away all tears from their eyes.

1) A Great Multitude out of the Great Tribulation
2) Celebrating the Feast of Tabernacles
3) Cry with a loud voice salvation belongs to our God.
4) Washed Their Robes and made them white in the Great Tribulation.
5) They are before the Throne of God serving as King/Priests day and night.
6) They hunger and thirst no more as have become immortal resurrected saints.
7) Are given the right to Kingdom of heaven Millennial age Rewards.

Take these seven major points of emphasis from the passage of Scriptures can any deny this rapture occurs during the Great Tribulation. Some Pretribulation teachers argue the Church does not appear after Revelation chapter four. However, passages which identify the Church at the seventh chapter, teaches a Great Multitude are brought from earth to Heaven after the sixth seal is opened. Other passages demonstrate Christians are persecuted and even martyred by refusing to take the mark of the Beast (Antichrist). In Revelation chapter twenty saints who were martyred refusing the mark are given crown and thrones to reign with Jesus Christ during the Millennial Kingdom age. Other passages identify the Church is overcome by the Antichrist for a season until the final judgment when Jesus Christ bursts forth with the armies of heaven.

Revelation 13:7-10 (50)
7 And it was given unto him to make war with the saints, and to
overcome them: and power wasgiven him over all kindr eds, and tongues, and nations.
8 And all that dwell upon the earth shall
worship him, whose names are not written in the
book of life of the Lamb slain from the foundation of the world.
9 If any man have an ear, let him hear.
10 He that leadeth into captivity shall
go into captivity: he that killeth with the sword must be killed with the sword. Here is the patience and the
faith of the saints.

The Church is clearly identified by this passage being called the saints. The Antichrist makes war with these Great Tribulation Christians, and has power over all kindreds, tongues, and nations, all who dwell upon the earth. The rule of the Antichrist during the Great Tribulation is universal, leading to the death or prison of

many Christians who remains and has been left behind after the first rapture.
So, we must not conclude every Christian is raptured with the Pre-Tribulation rapture as many are simply not prepared and are left behind in the heat of Tribulation Trials. Washing their robes white in the Blood of the Lamb which is conclusive proof these can only be identified as Christians, not Jews, or unbelievers. So, the evidence of Mid Tribulation, or Post Tribulation raptures where the Church is taken and removed by Rapture from earth to heaven is clearly recorded by Scriptures. A Great Multitude which no man can number is taken before the Throne of God after the opening of the sixth seal. This an enormous amount of people which likely includes both the living and dead saints. In the writing of Apostle Paul an order is given to the resurrection which teaches the dead in Christ rise first, followed by those who are alive and remain on earth. This is a picture of how the rapture(s) is connected to the first resurrection. As both the dead and living are gathered to the Lord in the air which are recorded as A Great Multitude come out of the Great Tribulation. The dead in Christ being raised first with the living saints to follow.

1 Corinthians 15:51-53 (51)
51 Behold, I shew you a mystery; We
shall not all sleep, but we shall all be changed,
52 In a moment, in the twinkling of an eye, at the
last trump: for the trumpet shall sound, and the dead

shall be raised incorruptible, and we shall be changed.
53 For this corruptible must put on incorruption
and this mortal must put on immortality.

This translation of the living saints at the coming of the Lord gathered with the dead in Christ is likely the explanation for the great numbers of saints taken before the Throne, after translation into immortality. In the rapture of living saints who are alive and remain at the coming "Parousia" of the Lord, are changed in a twinkling of an eye for mortality into immortality. So, the saints which appear before the Throne of God are resurrected immortal men not disembodied spirits who are still awaiting the resurrection. So, the order to the first resurrection first includes catching up of both the dead and living into the sky and the resurrection of their bodies into immortality at the same time.
See how Paul's writing to the Church at Thessalonians corresponds to the resurrection passage of Corinth. Paul teaches the dead saints proceeded the living in rapture, but both companies are taken at the "presence of the Lord," into the air and then taken before the Throne.

1 Thessalonians 4:13-18 (52)
13 But I would not have you to be
ignorant, brethren, concerning them which are
asleep, that ye sorrow not, even as others which
have no hope.

14 For if we believe that Jesus died and rose again, even so them also which sleep in Jesus will God
bring with him.
15 For this we say unto you by the word of the
Lord, that we which are alive and remain unto the coming of the Lord shall not prevent them which are asleep.
16 For the Lord himself shall
descend from heaven with a shout, with the voice of the archangel, and with the trump of God: and the
dead in Christ shall rise first:
17 Then we which are alive and remain shall be caught up together with them in the clouds, to meet the
Lord in the air: and so shall we ever be with the Lord.
18 Wherefore comfort one another with these words.

Between these two Scriptures is a confirmation rapture(s) precede the first resurrection. The Great Multitude in heaven which no man can number is both the dead saints and the living raptured and translated from mortality to immortality. Meeting the Lord at His Presence, appearing in the heavens at the Judgment Seat of Christ, also appearing before the Throne in heaven in their glorified immortal state. Those who were living saints did not prevent those who were dead in Christ, for the Lord shall descend from heaven with a shout, not all the way to the earth as in the Second Coming. Instead from the Throne to the clouds, and all those who are raptured at this time meet the Lord in the air. Do they then immediately descend with the

Lord back to earth? By no means for many more months will pass before the Lord bursts forth with the immortal glorified saints as the armies of heaven. Instead, the glorified saints are taken before the Throne from the air and are become immortal at the Judgment Seat of Christ.

What multiple raptures demonstrate is the rewards given to the faithful righteous, and even extend to the order of the resurrection. The prayerful and watching saints looking for the coming Parousia are considered the First Fruits of Harvest ripened before the others by righteous Godly living. The first fruits of harvest are the first in Rapture/Resurrection, the first to be judged at Christ's judgment Seat. The first in resurrection, and the first appear before the Throne as the glorified immortal sons of God. When do the sons of God manifest in the Day of Redemption? After their rapture, which is connected to their rewards and order to their resurrection. The first resurrection then is a series of raptures, where saints are immortalized according to the time of their being raptured or raised from the dead and taken before the Throne in heaven.

Chapter 9
The Rapture During Tribulation

Now after looking at the order of the first resurrection. First fruits rapture, then the Great Multitude in heaven. Let us take a further look at Scriptures which point to

the Rapture during the Tribulation. Paul writes to the Church of Thessalonians concerning the rapture at the time of the Antichrist.
(2 Thessalonians 2:1-3) 53
"Now we ask you, brothers, regarding the coming of our Lord Jesus Christ and our gathering together to Him, that you be not quickly shaken in mind nor alarmed, neither by a spirit nor by word nor by a letter as if by us, to the effect that the day of the Lord has come. Let no one deceive you in any way, because it will not come unless the apostasy comes first and the man of lawlessness is revealed, the son of perdition."

Here are the facts with the first fruits harvest the Lord does not descend but remains in Heaven. However, with the Great Multitude the Lord descends to the mid heavens in a cloud, and the Church ascends to the Lord in the clouds of the sky. The Scriptures put the rapture and the coming of the Lord together, at the time of the Antichrist, and the Great apostasy.

How can the saints know that the Day of the Lord had come as the Thessalonians wrongly believed? Some were saying the Lord had already come, and they were left behind to face the Great Tribulation. Paul sets the record straight; the Tribulation rapture will not occur until the Man of Lawlessness (Antichrist) is revealed and the Great Apostasy from the faith. It will be during this time the Lord will leave the throne of heaven and descend to the clouds of the sky to gather in the Great multitude of Harvest.

Now those who teach the Pre-Tribulation rapture of the whole Church use 2 Thessalonians to say the Day of the Lord means the Great Tribulation, as they reason the whole Church must be raptured before the Tribulation. Now instead the Scriptures reveal some Christians are raptured after the Great tribulation, or at least during a portion of it. As every Bible student aquatints the Great Tribulation with the coming of the Antichrist.

What Is the Last Trumpet?

Two trumpets are identified by Scriptures as the last Trumpet which signals the beginning of the events, or their ending. In 1 Thessalonians 4:16 the Trumpet sounded is for the "Great Multitude in Heaven Rapture," where Christ leaves His Throne to descend into the sky, to gather His saints in the clouds. As the Pre-Tribulation rapture happens without the Lord's descent, and is considered the first fruits rapture, not the harvest of the Great Tribulation.

1 Thessalonians 4:16 (54)
16 For the Lord himself shall
descend from heaven with a shout, with the voice of the archangel, and with the trump of God: and the
dead in Christ shall rise first:

The Lord descends to gather the Great Multitude with a shout, the voice of the arch angel, and with the Trump of God, which cannot be the same Trumpet as the last Trumpet, or the 7th Trumpet of Revelation. Instead, this Rapture is somewhere between the fifth and sixth seal and the Trumpet judgments are yet to sound.

Now the last Trumpet of Revelation 11:15 and 1 Corinthians 15:52 are likely the same Trumpet for the 7th Trumpet of Revelation is the last Trumpet. However, many judgments will happen under the 7th Trumpet, including the 7 Vials of Wrath. At the sounding of the Last Trumpet the resurrection of the righteous dead could signal this is the finality of the process of raptures, and the First Fruits, and Great Multitude. A process of their gathering unto the Lord, and their glorification into immortality. The final rapture would be all those who remained throughout the entire Great Tribulation like the gleanings of harvest. So, the last Trumpet in this case would signify the ending of the entire seven-year process.

We read in Revelation 11:15, "And the seventh angel sounded; and there were great voices in heaven, saying, 'The kingdoms of this world are become the kingdoms of our Lord, and of his Christ; and he shall reign for ever and ever.'" In the timetable of events the sounding of the seventh Trumpet occurs well into the tribulation period.

There is a difference being the between the rapture descent in 1 Thessalonians 4 which does not bring Jesus Christ all the way to earth at that point, but only into the clouds above the earth. While after the seventh Trumpet, the saints must be judged and arranged in heaven, transformed into immortality, before the glorified immortal saints can return with the Lord for the battle of Armageddon on earth. The descent of the Lord from heaven to earth does not happen until Revelation chapter 19, well after the 7th Trumpet of Revelation chapter 11 has been sounded.

The mystery of the last Trumpet then is best separated by its events. The trumpet sounded in Thessalonians is given in a moment, an instant of time. Whereas the trumpet voice of the seventh angel seems to sound throughout an extended period. (Revelation 10:7) Even though the 7th Trumpet is the last trumpet in the Book of Revelation, Paul's trumpet in Corinthians could possibly be another trumpet which ends the age with the finality of the first resurrection. As the Thessalonians passage deals with rapture, and the Corinthians passage deals with resurrection and transformation into immortality. The question which lies before us is at what time are the saints immortalized after Rapture and before the return of the Lord to the earth? Is a saint glorified upon rapture, each man entering immortality by stage, or are all saints immortalized at the same time, even though being raptured before others?

In 1 Corinthians 15, Paul is writing to believers concerning the transition from this life to eternal life. Our mortal bodies will be transformed into immortal, incorruptible bodies, prepared for entrance into the Millennial kingdom. Paul teaches the transformation happens in a moment, in the twinkling of an eye, at the last trump: for the trumpet shall sound, and the dead shall be raised incorruptible, and we shall be transformed. So are the order raptures first then glorification into immortality simultaneously, or rapture glorification, followed by the next rapture and glorification, until finally all who are Christ's are gathered with some who remain through the Great Tribulation transformed at the very end.

Many who teach the multiple rapture position teach "the saints cannot appear before God unclothed," that is without their glorified immortal bodies. So, all the scenes of raptured men in heaven, are raptured and immortalized at their time of rapture. So, this would put the first resurrection by order, Christ being the first, then the first fruits rapture, followed by the Great Multitude harvest, finally the gleanings of Great Tribulation saints. Every man taken by reward in his order of rapture and glorification.

In the Old Testament trumpets were used to set the people into the proper direction and assembly. In the

Book of Numbers chapter ten the first Trumpet blast assembled the leaders, while a continual blowing of the trumpet was a signal to alarm the believers. Also, different trumpet blasts into a serious brought each tribe of Israel into proper place and order. When all tribes had been assemblies in their order the "last trumpet blast was sounded." In Corinthians, the resurrection is described by Paul as each man having his rank, position, and order. In this way every saint is brought in order by rapture, and presented before the Lord for rewards of glorification, or loss of rewards. When all saints have been gathered before the Lord in rapture resurrection the last blast will have sounded. These are the Scriptural facts which Paul presents to the Church about our gathering unto the Lord, and immortalization.

Is the Last Trumpet Pre-Tribulation? The Scriptures never teach the last trumpet to be Pre-Tribulation . No man can produce Scriptures which demonstrate this position. Instead, the sounding of the last Trumpet, the 7th Trumpet is well into the Great Tribulation (3 ½ years). If Pre-Tribulation were the only rapture, why are seven more Trumpets sounded after Revelation chapter four? The Bible says the Last Trumpet is the Trumpet of God and signals the judgments of God. Christians need to examine to see if the last Trumpet in 1 Corinthians matches with the last Trumpet in Book of Revelation.

Revelation 10:7 (55)
7 But in the days of the voice of the
seventh angel, when he shall begin to sound, the
mystery Of God should be finished, as he hath
declared to his servants the prophets.

Left Behind Christians Are Raptured During Tribulation

Those who are left behind are also evidence of rapture after Tribulation. At first glance First Thessalonians might support the Pre-Tribulation position of rapture. After all, how can Scriptures teach the dead in Christ rise first followed by the living saints, if another rapture is to occur after this event?

1 Thessalonians 4:13-17 (56)

13 But I would not have you to be
ignorant, brethren, concerning them which are
asleep, that ye sorrow not, even as others which
have no hope.
14 For if we believe that Jesus died and rose again, even
so them also which sleep in Jesus will God
bring with him.
15 For this we say unto you by the word of the
Lord, that we which are alive and remain unto the
coming of the Lord shall not prevent them which are
asleep.

16 For the Lord himself shall
descend from heaven with a shout, with the voice of the
archangel, and with the trump of God: and the
dead in Christ shall rise first:
17 Then we which are alive and remain shall be caught
up together with them in the clouds, to meet the
Lord in the air: and so shall we ever be with the Lord.

Once again apostle Paul confirms an order to the rapture/resurrection. Notice this is the meeting of the Lord in the air? Which directly speaks of rapture, and in particular the rapture of the Great Harvest, where Christ leaves the Throne to the mid heavens in the sky. It is at this time the dead in Christ are said to have risen to meet the Lord, while the living saints follow. So, in referring to the living saints Paul puts a qualification, "those who are alive and remain," in other words. Some of those were alive had already left. However, the remaining living saints, who now would be taken at the time of gathering into the sky, will not precede the dead in Christ who are taken at this time before the living remaining saints.

In the first fruits harvest some of the living saints had already been taken and removed into heaven without the Lord descending from His throne. Now those saints who were not taken in the first fruits rapture are "those who are alive and remain," speaking of the Tribulation rapture. Some Pre-Tribulation saints had already been taken, while the remaining had been left behind to be taken later. Was this not the original concern of some

Thessalonians who felt they had missed the first resurrection rapture being left behind to face the Antichrist and Great Tribulation? Paul had said, the Antichrist and Great Apostasy must first appear before the Lord's descent from the Throne and the gathering in the sky.

The point being those who are alive and left behind or remain after the first fruits rapture are proof of a second rapture. Instead of proving all the Church taken in a Pre-Tribulation Rapture, this Scripture proves a Great Tribulation Rapture. Which also matches with the rapture teaching of Jesus Christ in Matthew chapter twenty-four of the Thief Like coming of the Lord.

Two major events must happen which qualify the Tribulation time spoken by Jesus Christ and confirmed by the apostle Paul. One is the Great Apostasy, the second is the coming of the Antichrist.

Chapter 10
Multiple Rapture Teachers

I hold to what is considered a "selective rapture position." Some of the Christian theologians which held and taught this position are: Watchman Née, G H Lang, George Peters, G H Pember, Joesph Seiss, Robert Govett and many others. Most of these men lived in the 1800's when the doctrine of the Millennial kingdom was being strongly taught and restored back into the

Church. The selective rapture position teaches a thief like coming of the Lord, to take only those saints who are watching and prayerful. With the rest of the saints who are sleeping and entangled with the world being left behind to experience a portion of the Tribulation trials.

The selective rapture doctrine has a Pretribulation, Mid Tribulation, and Post Tribulation rapture event. So, the selective rapture is also a multiple rapture belief. I trust very few Christians who hold to a literal rapture would hold to a selective rapture position. Most who believe in the Rapture are Pre-Tribulation with the entire Church being removed at that time. Christian men like Watchman Nee taught the selective rapture position extensively. I have been greatly affected by Watchman Nee's teachings on other subjects, even if in the beginning I would have not agreed with his selective rapture position. This is my hope for modern day Christians. Will take a Biblical examination on this doctrine and make a solid decision to prepare for the Second Coming of Jesus Christ.

Watchman Nee
Revelation 14:1-5 is on the first fruits; verses 6-13 are on the great tribulation (that is, the warning of the three angels); verses 14-16 are on the reaping of the wheat; and verses 17-20 are on the gathering of the grapes. When will the warning of the three angels occur? It will take place at the time of the great

tribulation. Therefore, the rapture of the first fruits in 14:1-5 will take place before the great tribulation, while the harvest of the wheat and the gathering of the grapes will take place after the great tribulation. What is the harvest? In the Bible it refers to the rapture. How do we know that the harvest of the wheat refers to the rapture? Because the wheat is gathered into the barn. The houses of the Jews were in one place and their fields were in another place. The barn is built near the house, and the wheat is stored in the barn, which is far away from the field but close to the house. Therefore, the barn is the air. Since the field is the world and the house is where God the Father dwells, the ripened wheat cannot be stored in either of the two places. Therefore, the barn must be the air. This is according to the significance of the harvest.
Collected Works of Watchman Nee, the (Set 1) Vol. 15: Study on Matthew, chapter 14 section 6. (57)

Without the way out mentioned in Luke 21:36, it would be impossible to understand many passages of the Bible. The rapture is a hidden thing, because the Bible says that the Lord will come as a thief (Matt. 24:43; 1 Thes. 5:4). This means that the Lord's coming is hidden and is not open. But then, on the other hand, the Bible says that we should not let the day come upon us as a thief, which means that the Lord's coming is open. On the one hand, it is hidden, and on the other hand, it is open. How can we explain this if there are not two comings of the Lord? How can we reconcile these two groups of Scriptures unless a small number of believers are raptured before the tribulation and most of them are raptured after the tribulation?

In addition to these verses, Revelation 12:5 speaks of being caught up to the throne of God. Revelation 14:3 says that these ones are before the throne. Luke 21:36 says that they will be placed before the Son of Man. All these refer to a rapture to heaven. But there are also other verses that speak of being raptured to the air. For example, 1 Thessalonians 4:17 says "to meet the Lord in the air," and Matthew 25:10 says, "The bridegroom came; and those who were ready went in with him to the wedding feast." This also happens in the air. The harvest in Revelation 14:14-16 also takes place in the air. If the rapture all takes place before the tribulation, or all after the tribulation, how can these two groups of verses be explained? Therefore, it is indeed a biblical teaching to say that a minority of the believers will be raptured before the tribulation, whereas most of them will be raptured after the tribulation. Otherwise, it would be impossible to explain many verses.

Moreover, the Bible says that no one knows the day of the coming of Christ. But at the same time, the Bible also says that the day of the coming of Christ can be known. On the one hand, it says that Christ will come at the sounding of the seventh trumpet, at the blowing of the last trumpet. On the other hand, it says, "concerning that day and hour, no one knows" (Matt. 24:36) and "at an hour when you do not expect it, the Son of Man is coming" (v. 44). If there is only one rapture, how can you not know His coming? Since the Bible has said that He will come at the blowing of the seventh trumpet, you can find out the time of Christ's coming by counting three and a half years from the time Antichrist begins sitting in Jerusalem. Why then does the Bible say that concerning that day and hour, no one knows? This means that some will be raptured before the tribulation, because no one knows the time of the rapture before the tribulation. But anyone can find out the time of the rapture after the tribulation. I dare not say that there are only two raptures. But I can say that according to the Bible, there is such a distinction in the rapture. On the one hand, it cannot be known, but on the other hand, it can be known. On the one hand, it is hidden, but on the other hand, it is open. On the one hand, men cannot see it, but on the other hand, many can see it. If we have any prejudice, it will be impossible for us to interpret these verses.

Collected Works of Watchman Nee, the (Set 1) Vol. 19: Notes on Scriptural Messages (3), Chapter 9, Section 5) (58)

G H Lange

Finally, as between the gathering of the sheaf of first-fruits and the ingathering of the harvest there came the intense summer heat, so between the removal of the

First-fruits and the reaping of the Harvest there is placed (ver. 9 - 13) the Great Tribulation, that final persecution which while, like all persecution, it will wither the unrooted stalk (Matt. 13: 21), ripens the matured grain. It is ripeness, not the calendar or the clock, that determines the time of reaping (Mk. 4: 29). The Heavenly Husbandman reaps no unripe grain: hence, "the hour to reap is come" when the harvest is "dried up" (Rev. 14: 15), for the dryness of the kernel in the husk is its fitness for the gamer and for use. Thus, the Great Tribulation will be a true mercy to the Lord's people by fully developing and sanctifying them for their heavenly destiny and glory.

It thus appears that the foretold order of events will be: -

1. The removal of such as prevail to escape the Times of the End. These will be taken up to God and to His [page 45 - THE FORETOLD ORDER] throne on the Mount Zion, not to the air. Nor does the Lord come for them; they are simply taken, like Enoch or Elijah taken to stand before Him and His throne. Nor is a resurrection announced for this moment. The dead, because dead, will have escaped the End-times, which escape is the announced object of this rapture.
   GH Lange First Fruits and Harvest Chapter 4 Pre-Tribulation Rapture (59)

Hudson Taylor

In the Appendix to his small work on The Song of Songs, entitled Union and Communion (ed. 5, p. 83), (60)

Hudson Taylor wrote of such as "if saved, are only half-saved:* who are for the present more concerned about the things of this world than the things of God. To advance their own interests, to secure their own comfort, concerns them more than to be in all things pleasing to the Lord. They may [page 29 - HUDDSON TAY4OR AND CHAPMAN] form part of that great company spoken of in Rev. 7: 9 - 17, who come out of the great tribulation, but they will hot form part of the 144,000, 'the first-fruits unto God and to the Lamb' (Rev. 14: 1-5). They have forgotten the warning of our Lord in Luke 21: 34 - 36; and hence they are not 'accounted worthy to escape all these things that shall come to pass, and to stand before the Son of Man.' They have not, with Paul, counted 'all things but loss for the excellency of the knowledge of Christ Jesus the Lord,' and hence they do not 'attain unto' that resurrection from among the dead, which Paul felt he might miss, but aimed to attain unto.

Robert Chapman

Robert Chapman about the year 1896 issued a series of Suggestive Questions. Number 10 includes the following: (61) "Are not the redeemed in Rev. 4 and 5 the same with those in ch. 20: 4, 'Thrones and they sat upon them'? (verse 5) 'This is the first resurrection.' Is it not a resurrection of first-fruits?" ... Now in the essential nature of the case first-fruits are but a portion of the whole harvest, and so the Question proceeds: 'And the rest of the dead (in the same verse) do they not include all the family of God? not the wicked dead only. Hence, in verse 12, 'Another book was opened, which is the book of life: and the dead were judged out of those things which were written in the books, according to their works' (verse 15). 'And whosoever was not found written in the book of life was cast into the lake of fire'."

Robert Govett

1. When the Son of God is come, the ready saints ascend to Him. When the Lord Jesus is come, the Hinderers depart. They cannot leave before that time, since otherwise the Day of wrath, and the Apostasy, would be assailing the Church. The Rapture of the ready ones precedes the Day of woe. The Hinderers must be removed before the Apostasy, and the Day of Judgment,

which avenges it. Thus, the Church and Spirit are seen to be the Hinderers.

2. Ambassadors are removed before war begins. The Church is God's ambassador, bearing His message of grace and peace. The Church then (I mean always the ready of the Church) must be removed before the war of God begins. Those left are discredited, and they keep not the Church's original standing. The removal of the Hinderers is the rapture of God's ambassadors, because the day of grace is over, and the day of judgment set in. The Holy Spirit and the ready of the Church depart together, for nearly the same reasons.

3. The Man of Sin is 'the Lawless One'. Until the ready saints are caught up to Christ's Presence, the Lawless One is not come, and cannot come. If the Hinderers are on earth, in the way of Satan's plans, so long the Lawless One is not come. The saints then are the Hinderers. The sin of man and the judgments of God are stayed while the Hinderers are here, and while the Church is owned as God's witness of salvation.
Robert Govett; The Parousia of Christ; The Hinders. (62)

J A Seiss

One very striking statement in the Epistle to the Church at Philadelphia concerning those Christians who shall be alive at the Second Advent of Christ, and who shall be "keeping the word of His patience," is that they are to be "kept out of the hour of temptation" - out of that [Great Tribulation] season of trial, which is then to come upon the whole world, to try those who dwell upon the earth instead of cherishing a heavenly citizenship. (See [Rev.] chap. 3: 10.) How this deliverance is to be wrought, St. Paul explains. The saints, both living and resurrected*, [* There is no mention of a resurrection of the dead at this time. – Ed.] are to be miraculously snatched away from earth to heaven, suddenly, and in the twinkling of an eye. His own unmistakable words are: "Then we who are living, who remain, shall be caught up together with them (the resurrected ones) in the clouds, to meet the Lord in the air." (1 Thess. 4: 17.) The Saviour Himself has also given assurances to the same effect, where He says. "I tell you, in that night there shall be two in one bed: the one shall be taken, and the other shall be left. Two women shall he grinding together: the one shall be taken, and the other shall be left. Two shall be in the field: the one shall be taken, and the other left. And they answered and said unto Him, Where [or Whither], Lord? And He said unto them, Wheresoever the body is, thither will the eagles be gathered together." (Luke 17: 34-37.) And to this same marvelous occurrence, which Paul Speaks

of as one of the great mysteries (1 Cor. 15: 51), do the words at the head of this discourse refer. "I saw," says John, "and behold, a door set open in the heaven, and the former voice which I heard as of a trumpet, speaking with me, saying, Come up hither." That door opened in heaven is the door of the ascension of the saints. That trumpet voice is the same which Paul describes as recalling the sleepers* in Jesus. And that "Come up HITHER" is for everyone in John's estate, even the gracious and mighty word of the returning Lord Himself, by virtue of which they that wait for Him shall renew their strength and mount up with wings as eagles. (Isa. 40: 3l.) And thus, as the Psalmist sting, the Lord will hide them in the secret place of His presence from the vexation of man, and screen them in a tabernacle from the contradiction of tongues. (Psa. 31: 19, 20.)
JA Seiss; The Apocalypse Seventh Lecture (63)

And such is the next great scene which may now be any day expected. I know of nothing in the prophecies of God, unless it should be the mere deepening of the signs that have already appeared, which yet remains to be fulfilled before this sudden summons [of the watchful and "accounted worthy" saints] from the skies: "Come, My people, enter thou into thy chambers, and shut thy doors about thee: hide thyself as it were a little moment, until the indignation be overpast; for, behold, the Lord cometh out of His place to punish the inhabitants of the earth for their iniquity." (Isa. 26: 20, 21.) Any one of these days or nights, and certainly before many more years have passed, all this shall be accomplished. Some of these days or nights, - while men are busy with the common pursuits and cares of life, and everything is rolling on its accustomed course, - unheralded, unbelieved, and unknown to the gay world, here one, and there another, shall secretly disappear, "caught up" like Enoch, who "was not found because God had translated him." Invisibly, noiselessly, miraculously, they shall vanish from the company and fellowship of those about them and ascend to their returning Lord. Strange announcements shall be in the morning papers of missing ones. Strange accounts shall be whispered around in the circles of business and society. And for the first time will apostate Christendom, and the slow in heart to believe all that the prophets have written, have the truth brought home, that no such half-Christianity as theirs is sufficient to put men among the favorites of the Lord.

Brethren and friends, these are neither dreams nor fables. They are realities, set forth in the infallible truth of God, and as literally true as anything else in the inspired Word. And as you value the prize of our high calling in Christ Jesus, and take this holy book as an unfailing guide, be not faithless, but believing.* And if you feel yourself unready for such events, do not think of setting them aside by scoffs and sneers.

J A Seiss; The Apocalypse: Seventh Lecture (64)

GNH Peters

Obs. 4. Other passages either directly teach such a translation or removal, or else strongly imply it as a resultant or prerequisite. Take Rev. 14, and the order of events is in the highest degree corroborative of our position. Without discussing the relation that this chapter sustains to previous predictions, it is sufficient for our present purpose to notice that a time arrives before the final end when a certain specified number of saints, viz., the 144,000 (a symbolic number?) mentioned, are separated from among men, forming a chosen body called "the first-fruits unto God and to the Lamb" These "first-fruits' go before the incoming harvest, an interval of time (which includes (1) the proclamation of the particular message that God's judgments are to be poured out, and insisting upon the worship of God in view of the Antichristian worship that will be required; (2) the downfall of Babylon, and (3) the fearful persecution and martyrdom of believers) being placed between the two, at the close of which the harvest comes, and the dreadful vintage follows. This teaches us then to expect that a gathering of saints before the harvest is indeed one of the Divine procedures pertaining to the last things of this dispensation. The Parable of the Ten Virgins (Prop. 181) confirms this, for it instructs (aside from other particulars) us to anticipate at the Coming of Jesus that a certain class of persons (called the Wise Virgins in contradistinction to another class pronounced the Foolish), living at the time of the Sec. Advent, shall be so fortunate, owing to preparedness, as to be received, by Jesus Christ at His Coming, while others shall be left. The adverb of time "then" binds this parable to the preceding context and forces us to interpret it as a representation of the condition of the Church at some distinctive point of the Sec. Advent. Without insisting upon the explanation given by Olshausen, Alford, Stier, Seiss, etc., that the foolish virgins are even persons of some piety, who, neglecting to look for the Bridegroom, are left to endure the incoming tribulation, it is amply sufficient to say that the persons left are, at least, professing members of the Church, and that, as the announcement of the marriage (Rev. 19) precedes the overthrow of the Antichristian powers, those left behind must necessarily endure the trials incident to the arrogance, etc., of those powers. Those going into the marriage—living saints taken away, translated, for this purpose—precede the time of sore tribulation. Passages which imply it relate to the promised participation of the saints in acts of judgment upon the living nations, to the married wife as distinguished from the barren woman, to the coming with the saints for purposes of salvation, etc. But others of a still stronger tenor are embraced in the promises that when the last great tribulation is to burst upon the Gentile nations, then certain believing ones shall escape. Thus e.g., Luke 21: 36, "Watch ye therefore and pray always, that ye may be accounted worthy to escape all these things that shall come to pass and to stand before the Son of Man the escaping and being favored with nearness to Christ are united. In Rev. 3: 10, of a class it is said: "Because thou hast kept the word of my patience, I also will keep thee from the hour of temptation (or trial) which shall come upon the world, to try them that dwell upon the earth." The 144,000 described above are taken from this "the hour of trial," comp. Rev. 14: 7. It is a joyful fact that when the most fearful time of trial, the flood of great waters, comes, then God interposes in behalf of His own people and saves them out of it (to which even such passages as Ps. 32: 6, 7; Prov. 3: 25, 26; Ps. 37: 38-40, etc., may refer), while another class are left to endure its terrific force and come up out of it as blood-stained martyrs, Rev. 14: 9-13; Rev. 20: 4, 5, etc. It is significant also that in Rev. 7 we have first a distinct, separate number of chosen ones forming the same number, 144,000 (called Jews, because engrafted by faith and thus incorporated with the commonwealth), and then afterward a great multitude who come "out of the great tribulation,"' thus again pointing out a distinction existing between certain of God's people. Such are not given without adequate causes, and it is well to heed them.

The Theocratic Kingdom GNH Peters: Proposition 130: The Kingdom Is Preceded by the Translation of the Living Saints (65)

GH Pember

But the Lord has not thought of translating worldly-minded believers from the toils of life into the joys of His presence, of admitting them to immorality by the gate of glory instead of the dark valley of death. Those who vainly expect such a thing are like the Jews, who would have had Christ put Himself at their head as the all-victorious King, when yet He had not saved them from their sins. But He will not grant to the careless and slothful servant that blessing which Paul craved, yet did not receive (2 Cor. 5: 2-4) - the joy of being clothed upon, without the necessity of shuffling off this mortal coil. Hence in His promise to the Philadelphians, He says: "Because thou didst keep the word of My patience, - [Gk. "the word of the endurance ,"] - I will also keep thee from the hour of trial, that hour, which is to come upon the whole world, to try them that dwell upon the earth" (Rev. 3: 10).

It thus appears that not all believers will be caught up to the Lord at the commencement of His second Advent, [3] but only those who are found watching. It is, indeed, true that Paul, after speaking of Christ's descent into the air, adds: "Then we which are alive and remain shall be caught up," without any mention of exceptions to the rule (1Thess. 4: 16, 17). But other Scriptures show that His words are to be regarded as a general statement, expressing what ought to be, and potentially may be, the case with every Christian. Similarly, in another place, he says: "It is appointed unto men once to die": yet the very next verse reveals the secret that some will escape death. And in this first Epistle to the Corinthians, he discloses the mystery that we shall not all sleep.

Just in the same general way the Lord said to His disciples, "Verily, I say unto you, that ye which have followed Me . . . ye shall also sit upon twelve thrones, judging the twelve tribes of Israel." But Judas had followed Him, and was at the time one of the twelve: will he also occupy a throne in the regeneration? Nay, we know from the authority of Scripture that his own "place", to which he went, was in realms of the lost.

With the current foolishly optimistic view - that as soon as we believe we are in possession of all the glorious possibilities that are set before us - it is not strange that Christians neglect the admonition to pass the time of their sojourning in fear (1Pet. 1: 17); that they ignore the warning, "Many are called, but few chosen" (Matt. 22: 14); and that they are not rendered anxious even by the thought that those only who are accounted worthy shall escape the things that are coming to pass, and shall obtain the Millennial Age and the resurrection [out] from the dead.

THE COMING TRANSLATION OF WATCHFUL CHRISTIANSG. H. Pember, M.A. (66)

F W Roadhouse

Remembering that the Revelation shows two historical points where there is rapture - at the middle of the seven years and at the end - we find that here (in 20: 4) there are two groups. The first is already set (5: 4, first part); the second is here described in detail. They are, of course, the 'first fruits' and the 'harvest', as shown in chapter 14: 4, 15where the very expressions are used. Together these two installments make the one harvest. (1) The First-fruits Wave Sheaf rose 1,900 years ago (Christ). Now the first-fruits Wave loaves, three- and one-half years before the [Millennial] Kingdom. (2) To complete those first fruits, the harvest company is added - namely, the victors over 'the beast' and his image and his mark (as we saw in chapter 13.). These combine to make 'the First resurrection' (20: 4). For the type above, see Leviticus 23: 10, 17, 22.

Why are they already seen enthroned, this first cited company? Because, as chapter 12. shows, when Satan was cast out of heaven forty-two months before, 'a loud voice' was heard saying, "Now is come the salvation, and the power, and the kingdom of our God, and the authority of our Christ." With this went the formula that John ever uses to describe the Overcomers, "And they overcame him (Satan) because of the blood of the Lamb, and because of the word of their testimony, and they loved not their lives unto the death" - a threefold

qualification. And these Overcomers were already, in some degree, taken up into the heavenly place of regency. Together with their Great Overcomer, the "First-born out of the dead" (1: 5), these first fruits were already "caught up unto God and His throne" 1,260 days ere the Kingdom came into world visibility.
[* The following is taken from Mr. Panton's Evangelical Magazine - (THE DAWN, vol. 13., No. 9, December 15th. 1936.) (67)

Other Notable Theologians

For example, Christ's parable of the "Ten Virgins" in Matthew 25 (like so many of His other parables) spawned multitudes of accountability teachers. In his own comments upon the parable, Joseph Seiss (1823-1904) quotes Olshausen as stating: "The words 'I know you not,' cannot denote eternal condemnation. The foolish virgins are only excluded from the Marriage of the Lamb... but are not thereby deprived of eternal happiness.'...." 11 Seiss agrees with this view. George N.H. Peters attests to the fact that this was also the view of Poiret, Von Meyer, Rudolph, Stier, Bayford, and others. 12 Seiss continues: "Stier also agrees that 'a further hope as regards the last end must remain.' Dean Alford also concurs in the same. So too, the Theological and Literary Journal, in an article on this parable.... The same view is also maintained by Poiret... Von Mayer... and others." 13 Again, "and others" is an understatement. The view appears to have almost dominated premillennial thought by the middle of the nineteenth century. Many early scholars held to the belief that the Foolish Virgins are ultimately saved, though excluded temporarily from either the pre-trib rapture or the millennium, or both. Early influential writers such as William Cuninghame (1775-1849) and some of the other Albury Park (1826-28) scholars (among whom the pre-trib rapture and secret coming revived in the mainstream), held to the belief that the Foolish Virgins are ultimately saved, though excluded temporarily. Other early, prominent scholars who held this view of the Virgins include Thomas Evill, Tilson Marsh, John Cumming, Charles D. Maitland (1830), J. Hooper, Robert Polwhele, J. Coleman, Colonel Rowlandson, C. Beale, R.A. Purdon, D.N. Lord, J. Echlin, E. Bickersteth, etc. Many applied this exclusion to the whole millennial age.

Philip Schaff in Lange's Commentary on Matthew 68
Joseph Augustus Seiss, The Parable of The Ten Virgins (1862). 69
George N.H. Peters, The Theocratic Kingdom, vol. 3 (Grand Rapids: Kregel), 306. 70

Excerpt from: The Rod Will God Spare It: Kindle Position Chapter 26 Accountability Truth in History pt. 1) 71

Oswald Jeffery Smith
Smith: "…' If we suffer, we shall also reign with Him.' This was the great incentive to the Christians of the early Church.… Pastor D.M. Panton, widely known

writer and diligent student of prophecy... Hudson Taylor and others have been exponents of 'select' or 'partial' rapture and a 'partial' reign. This view I must say I have no hesitation whatever in accepting."
Oswald J. Smith, Is the Antichrist at Hand? (Tabernacle Publishers, 1927) 72

Chapter 11
Rapture: The Escape into Safety

What are the Scriptural evidence Christians desire to be removed from the coming Great Tribulation by rapture? In the multiple rapture doctrine those Christians who are left behind must go through a measure of the Great Tribulation. It is also where many who refuse the Mark of the Beast, are martyred for their faith in Christ. The Scriptures also demonstrate Christians who miss the first fruits rapture, did not prepare themselves sufficiently needing to wash the robes white during the Tribulation. Missing the first rapture points towards a lack of prayer and watchfulness, while being caught up in the things of the world. In many respects an element of reward or loss of reward is involved in being taken or left behind. Here are 4 factors to consider about the first fruits rapture and the escape into safety.

1) Escape from God's catastrophic Judgments.
2) Escape from Antichrist martyrdom
3) Escape from the Great Apostasy
4) Escape into Holiness and Rewards

The Tribulation begins when Jesus Christ receives the 7 Sealed Book of Judgment as written in Revelation chapter five. The first four seals are the release of the four horsemen of the Apocalypse and are the beginning of the judgment of God which ends up with the 7th seal, and the 7 Bowls of God's wrath. Sometimes those who teach the Pretribulation rapture is an escape from responsibility have misunderstood the nature of the Tribulation. They teach the Tribulation will be a time of a great harvest of souls, however, the exact opposite is written by Scriptures. During the time of the Tribulation the world will not be coming to saving faith, instead will embrace the false Messiah, and mock the Christian faith. The Scriptures record the time of Tribulation is also the time of the Great Apostasy, a departure from the faith.

Preceding the Tribulation will come a time of lawlessness where iniquity will abound. The Scriptures warn the love of many Christians will grow cold because of the lawless spirit which is being embraced and celebrated throughout the world. The moral decline is likened to the Days of Noah and the time of Lot in Sodom. The people of the world will be completely lost and blinded to the impending catastrophic judgments which God is about to execute all over the world. The conditions are very "antichrist," and reflect the hatred the world has for Jesus Christ and true believers. Jesus Christ also warned the authentic Church will be hated by every nation before the Second Coming, so persecution against Christians will be very great. Also, deception will be very present in the numbers of false Christ's and false prophets which will arise with the coming of the Antichrist. Instead of leading great masses of peoples to faith in Jesus Christ, quite the opposite will manifest as Christians will be tempted to abandon the faith.

Jesus Christ also warns the change which comes when those who hinder the coming of the Antichrist are removed off the scene. The Bible teaches "the hinders" help keep back the tide of the antichrist spirit, until the appointed time and then will be taken out of the way. Who or what then are those who hinder until they are removed by God? Some teach it is the removal of the Holy Spirit, so gross darkness can come and take over. However, I trust this is a weak argument at best, for is there anywhere the Spirit of God is not present? Maybe some of the influences of the Holy Spirit are set aside, but I think the removal of the hinders is not the removal of God the Holy Spirit.

Instead, the removal is those who restrain ungodly influences in the world by being the light and salt of the earth. It seems more likely the removal of the first fruits harvest by Pre-Tribulation rapture releases an increase in wickedness and darkness. Some Christians have a great influence against evil by their Godly dedication, and witness to the life of Christ. Those who qualify for

the first fruits harvest, are called over comers by Jesus Christ in the Book of Revelation. Those men and women whose lives shine as a great light, their lamps burning bright, are also chaste virgins in Jesus Christ.
Overcoming Christians are the light and salt of the earth keeping corruption in check by their Godly works of faith.

2 Thessalonians 2:6-9 (73)
6 And now ye know what withholdeth that he might be revealed in his time.
7 For the mystery of iniquity doth already work: only he who now letteth will let, until he be taken out of the way.
8 And then shall that Wicked be revealed, whom the Lord shall consume with the spirit of
his mouth, and shall destroy with the brightness of
his coming:
9 Even him, whose coming is after the working of Satan with all power and signs and lying wonders,

For the mystery of iniquity does already work, only he who now let us will let, until he shall be taken out of the way. (2 Thessalonians 2:7) The mystery of inquiry, the works of darkness, false religions, antichrist worship, as characterized by Mystery Babylon in Revelation is allowed by God. Now the removal of the hider's is supported by the rapture of the first fruits into the Throne room of God. At the same time of their rapture, Satan is cast out of the second heaven, onto the earth having great wrath knowing his time is short. It appears with the casting out of Satan by the first fruits rapture, then the Antichrist is reveled. If this be the event of the removal of the hinders, the first fruits rapture, and the coming of the Antichrist, then the passage is easily understood by comparing Revelation chapter 12 with 2 Thessalonians chapter 2.

Revelation 12:5-9 (74)
5 And she brought forth a man child, who was
to rule all nations with a rod of iron: and her child was caught up unto God, and to his throne.
6 And the woman fled into the wilderness, where She hath a place prepared of God, that they should
feed her there a thousand two
hundred and threescore days.
7 And there
was war in heaven: Michael and his angels fought agains t the dragon; and the Dragon fought and his angels,
8 And prevailed not; neither was their place found any more in heaven.
9 And the great dragon was cast out, that
old serpent, called the Devil, and Satan, which deceives the world: he was cast out into the
earth, and his angels were cast out with him.

Now with the removal of the man child, the first fruits harvest rapture unto the Throne of God accompanies a war in the heavens. With the first fruits harvest taking Satan's right of place, overcoming Christians as kings and priests ascend in rapture into the Throne room of heaven. Satan is displaced and with the dark angels being cast out of the mid heavens unto the earth, for the final battle on earth in this age called, Armageddon. Some believe the casting out of Satan from the mid heavens to earth is also the incarnation of Satan into the man who is the Antichrist. Whoever, the Antichrist might be, it appears he is healed of a mortal wound which could explain the possession of Satan. At any rate, the Antichrist is the world's false Messiah who imitates the resurrection. So, Satan is a big part of producing the lying signs and wonders which leads the world to worship the Antichrist.

With all these considerations in place Christians need to see how rapture is promised as a reward of escape for the over comer in Christ. It is never taught by Scripture as an escape into avoidance of responsibility, or the neglect of the Great Commission. On the contrary the first fruits are Chaste Virgins in Christ, holy, prayerful and the light and salt of the earth. Those who influenced the world as a preserving agent, letting their lamps burn bright as a faithful witness to Jesus Christ. Those Christians who accuse the Pre-Tribulation rapture as escapism do so by neglecting the testimony of Scriptures.

Now the escape of reward, a protection from the Tribulation is what the Scriptures teach about the first fruits rapture. The protection must be from the coming judgments of God, and the opening of the 7 Sealed Book. Escape by Pre-Tribulation rapture is promised to the faithful. As previously stated, the time of the Tribulation is likened to the Days of Noah. The whole earth was filled with violence and the thought of man was continuously evil. How did God deliver His own? Noah and family were taken above the waters of judgment in the Ark of refuge. Above from God's impending judgment on earth above the great deluge of waters. Did God cause Noah to go through the judgments, or remove Him to safety by providing an ark of refuge? The whole world of humanity was destroyed by the flood waters of judgment, while Noah and his family were taken "above the flood." The ark was a refuge from God's judgment, so also is the first fruit rapture. Later God removes the Great Multitude gathering them to the Lord in the sky, so as not to partake in the wrath of God. (7 Vials of Wrath)

Judgments reign on earth with massive loss of life while God removes the faithful saints from harm's way by rapture. So, the first rapture is like an Ark of refuge, saints being taken into the Throne room of God far above the earth's greatest Tribulation since creation even unto the end. Rapture is the reward of rescue the faithful being taken, the unfaithful left behind. The warnings of being left behind are the loss of reward and are for purification of saints by the world's trials of end time judgments. It is very apparent as judgment falls upon the waters and land, or even in the heavens,

Christians who are left behind will suffer losses too. To what extent can only be hypothesized, but real suffering and loss will occur. Not the loss of salvation, instead the loss of privileges which come with faithful devotion and holiness.

Rapture provides protection and escape from Antichrist persecution, or even martyrdom. The fact of Scriptures demonstrate the Antichrist will for a season during the Great Tribulation make war with the saints and overcome them. Here are some Scriptures which demonstrate this coming reality:

Revelation 12:10-12 (75)
10 And I heard a loud voice saying in heaven, Now is come salvation, and strength, and kingdom
of God, and the power of his Christ: for the accuser of our brethren is cast down, which accused
them before our God day and night.
11 And they overcame him by the blood of the Lamb, and by the word of their testimony; and they loved not their lives unto the death.
12 Therefore rejoice, ye heavens, and ye that dwell in them. Woe to the inhabiters of the earth and of the sea! for the devil is come
down unto you, having great wrath, because he knoweth that he hath but a short time.

These Scriptures demonstrate the intense hatred Satan executes towards Christians who are present during the

Great Tribulation. Christians who are present during the Great Tribulation must be willing to accept martyrdom at the hands of Antichrist satanic hate. Saints left behind face the world's Tribulation and face the false Messiah who overcomes the saints. The saints of these days must overcome by the blood of the Lamb, the word of their testimony, and not loving their lives even unto death. In essence Tribulation saints must pick up the Cross and follow Jesus Christ into the fellowship of His sufferings.

Revelation 13:5-10 (76)
5 And there was given unto him a mouth speaking great things and blasphemies; and power was given unto him to continue forty and two months.
6 And he opened his mouth in blasphemy against God, to blaspheme his name, and his tabernacle, and them that dwell in heaven.
7 And it was given unto him to make war with the saints, and to overcome them: and power was given him over all kindreds, and tongues, and nations.
8 And all that dwell upon the earth shall worship him, whose names are not written in the book of life of the Lamb slain from the foundation of the world.
9 If any man have an ear, let him hear.
10 He that leadeth into captivity shall go into captivity: he that killeth with the

sword must be killed with the sword. Here is the patience and the faith of the saints.

Let us look at the facts during the forty-two moths of Antichrist rule. First the Antichrist will blasphemy God, and the saints both in heaven and on earth. The Antichrist will make war with the saints left on earth. Now will the saints then conquer the Antichrist by the power of God. No, just the opposite will happen, the Antichrist will rule over all the earth making war with the saints and overcome them. Only those saints who have not been removed by the first rapture, remain to face the horrific trail of their faith. God will allow saints to be incarcerated, to be put to death most by the sword being martyred for their faith. Tribulation saints will have to reject the mark, not worship the image of the Antichrist even unto death. While those who were raptured in the Pre-Tribulation first fruits ascent into the Throne room are removed completely from Antichrist warfare. This is the promised reward for the faithful in Christ.

Now to accuse Christians of fleeing responsibility, and not engaging the Great Commission because of a rapture mentality does not fit with the authority of Scriptures. As the Church is commanded by the Lord to watch and pray so all these things just previously mentioned does not come upon you. This is the council of Scriptures do not escape from responsibility. There are two realities which the Church will face during the time of the rapture(s). First the condition of worldliness over taking Christians is warned about, so also the Church falling asleep, and not watching in prayer caught up by the cares of this life. Second, the time of the Tribulation is not a time of massive conversions into the Christian faith. Instead, the Scriptures warn of the exact opposite, a great falling away from the faith into apostasy.

The conditions stated by Scripture are lawlessness will abound and the agape love of many Christians will have grown cold. Also, deception will abound with false prophets, false messengers (apostles), and lying signs and wonders. If possible, even the very elect will be tempted with deception. The moral conditions of the day will be like the time of Noah before the Great Flood where the thought of mankind was continuously evil, and bloodshed and violence filled the whole earth. Homosexuality will be practiced and widely celebrated, as well as all manner of sexual perversity. Instead of the Church being the light and salt of the earth, the Scriptures demonstrate the Church will be being trampled underfoot by its corrupted doctrines, and compromised faith. The Cross of Jesus Christ will be pushed aside to make way for the Christian fables which will be celebrated as the Gospel truth. The Church will be corrupted by the world, prayer less, Cross less, Christians, having lost its salt. Jesus Christ warned when the Christian faith had lost its salt (witness), it would be good for nothing except to be cast out and trampled underfoot by man.

Now this is Scriptural fact and troubles those Christian teachers who preach the Lord will not return for a defeated Church. Instead, they insist the Church will spread the glory of the Lord all over the world making the nations Christian before Jesus Christ can return. The doctrine of Kingdom Now/Dominion Theology has dominated the thinking of many Charismatics, who are teaching the Church will cleanse the pillars of culture making Christian nations. Afterwards the Lord will return to a world "already cleaned up and saved by the Church." This is the same camp which insists all of God's judgments are past, and only a golden age of the Church remains before the Second Coming of the Lord. The Dominion, Kingdom Now worldwide Church take over Charismatic crowd who refuse the council of Scripture, and instead insert their own will and philosophy in its place. They insist there is no rapture, and even mock those Christians who speak of a coming Great Tribulation.

Tribulation A Great End Time Harvest

In the Charismatic Movement many prophets have prophesied a great end time revival before the Second Coming of the Lord. The prediction is over one billion souls will come into saving faith by the greatest revival the world has ever seen. However, is there any

Scriptural proof the world's greatest salvation revival will happen right before the Second Coming of the Lord? The answer is simply no. Instead, the Bible speaks of a coming Great Tribulation, of the likes the world has never seen before. Also, in conjunction with the Great Tribulation, is a Great Apostasy from the Faith. Instead of massive salvation of a billion souls, the Bible predicts a Great Falling Away a massive denial of the faith.

2 Thessalonians 2:3-4 (77)
3 Let no man deceive you by any means: for that day shall not come, except there come a falling away first, and that man of sin be revealed, the son of perdition.
4 Who opposeth and exalteth himself above all that is called God, or that is worshipped; so that he as God sitteth in the temple of God, shewing himself that he is God.

The Bible also predicts a massive harvest of the Grapes of Wrath at the Second Coming of Jesus Christ. Instead of the Church becoming a Glorious Church without spot or wrinkle, the Church brings into fruition the demonic sons who are called tares by the Scriptures. It is at the time of the end the tares are separated out from the wheat and placed into a great fiery furnace. The harvest of the end of the age is one of God's wrath and judgments of the nations, not a massive conversion of souls into the Christian faith. Perhaps the false notion of end time revival has fed the demise of American Christianity and its massive departure from Bible morality. The Church has been locked away behind the four walls of Charismatic conferences will little to no actual making of new disciples through active evangelism.

Instead of massive revival America is in a massive departure into pagan religions, New Age, occultism, and Satanic Worship. It is time to wake up to reality, the war is happening right inside the Church with deception. The spirit of antichrist has brought in manmade philosophy holding the Church captive. Building Christian organizations and making millionaires of modern-day apostles is not the fulfillment of the Great Commission. Christians gathering in Mega Churches to hear a watered-down Gospel, or even worse is not the evidence of a great revival in America.
Now many will say the Great Tribulation is the time of a great revival. Instead, the Bible predicts men will openly worship Satan, and the Antichrist. This massive acceptance of devil worship is demonstrated by the peoples, tongues and nations taking the Mark of the Beast. The Scriptures declares anyone who takes the Mark of the Beast "cannot be saved." instead at the Coming of Jesus Christ will be cast into the Lake of Fire, along with the Antichrist and False Prophet.

Is what is the true picture of the coming Tribulation, a great revival, or a Great Apostasy? The Bible shows men who worship the Antichrist will have no opportunity to repent. Instead, they will harden their hearts against

God in rebellion and blasphemy. Men will rebel to the very end, to their own demise, for the nations who refuse the Lord will be turned into Hell. The true picture of the last days is characterized by mankind's total depravity and love of darkness. Not a billion-soul harvest, instead billions of souls brought under God's judgments and wrath.

Revelation 9:13-21 (78)

13 And the sixth angel sounded, and I heard a voice from the four horns of the golden altar, which is before God,
14 Saying to the sixth angel which had the trumpet, Loose the four angels which are bound in the great river Euphrates.
15 And the four angels were loosed, which were prepared for an hour, and a day, and a month, and a year, for to slay the third part of men.
16 And the number of the army of the horsemen were two hundred thousand thousand: and I heard the number of them.
17 And thus I saw the horses in the vision, and them that sat on them, having breastplates of fire, and of jacinth, and brimstone: and the heads of the horses were as the heads of lions; and out of their mouths issued fire and smoke and brimstone.
18 By these three was the third part of men killed, by the fire, and by the smoke, and by the brimstone, which issued out of their mouths.

19 For their power is in their mouth, and in their tails: for their tails were like unto serpents, and had heads, and with them they do hurt.
20 And the rest of the men which were not killed by these plagues yet repented not of the works of their hands, that they should not worship devils, and idols of gold, and silver, and brass, and stone, and of wood: which neither can see, nor hear, nor walk:
21 Neither repented they of their murders, nor of their sorceries, nor of their fornication, nor of their thefts.

Chapter 12
What Is the Great Apostasy?

In Paul's day the Christians of the Church of Thessalonians felt they had missed the first rapture and were left behind to face the Tribulation. However, the apostle Paul made a distinction between the suffering of the first century saints under Roman persecution, and the coming Tribulation. Apostle Paul noted the Tribulation time had not yet come, as the Great apostasy, the falling away from the faith was to coordinate with this time.

Now through the Church age there has been a great deal of departure from the authentic Christian faith. One of the major contributing factors was the rise of Catholicism and the Catholic Church. When Emperor Constantine declared Christianity to be the religion of the state, pagan principles were incorporated by the

Church of Rome into the Christian faith. In this way the paganism of the Christian faith has existed for over 1500 years. This, however, is not the Great Falling Away which Paul was teaching about in Thessalonica. Instead, this is the generalized attack of Christian doctrine, and departure from the orthodoxy of the original apostles teaching.

Today we have Protestant versions of doctrinal departure, and the introduction of man-made traditions, and human philosophy. In this way the authentic Christian faith has been attacked for a long time over the centuries by Protestant denominations also. Church history has proven what Jesus Christ warned is happened. The wheat and tares will grow side-by side during the Church age until the time of harvest at the end of the age. It is at the time of Tribulation the harvest will begin, where the wheat will be separated out from the tares by rapture and resurrection. It is also during the time of Tribulation which Paul speaks a great worldwide departure from the faith will occur called the Great Falling Away. Here are the passages which inform us of the Great End time Apostasy.

2 Thessalonians 2:1-3 (79)
1 Now we beseech you, brethren, by the coming of our Lord Jesus Christ, and by our gathering together unto him,

2 That ye be not soon shaken in mind, or be troubled, neither by spirit, nor by word, nor by letter as from us, as that the day of Christ is at hand.
3 Let no man deceive you by any means: for that day shall not come, except there comes a falling away first, and that man of sin be revealed, the son of perdition.

What leads Christians into the Great Apostasy

The Scriptures warn of great end time deception which leads the Church into the Great Apostasy. By its very definition apostasy can only be committed by those who first believed and then turned from the faith. So, Christians who have made a faith commitment to Jesus Christ, and then turned away from the faith, and even denying the Lord is the sin of apostasy. In the last days, the pressure to apostatize from the faith will become very great. Conditions from both inside the Church and outside the Church will lead Christians away into apostate conditions.
The apostle Paul in many of his writings speaks and warns of end time deception and apostasy. Paul said the influences from inside the Church will come from 1) false teachers, 2) Doctrines of demons, and 3) Immorality in the lives of Christians.

1 Timothy 4:1-2 (80)
1 Now the Spirit speaketh expressly, that in the latter times some shall depart from the faith, giving heed to seducing spirits, and doctrines of devils.

2 Speaking lies in hypocrisy; having their conscience seared with a hot iron.

In this passage the influences come from corrupted leaders who teach Christians man made wisdom, doctrines which deny the faith which come from evil spirits. The seducing spirits are the teachers themselves who seek to use the Church from the own personal profit and gain.

Again, in Paul's second letter to Timothy, the issue of end time peril is brought to the forefront. Paul includes how evil men and imposters have invaded the Church whose immorality is corrupting the household of faith. Paul uses the definition of perilous times as the Christian faith is being drawn away by corrupted leaders, false doctrines, and immoral practices. Paul teaches the leaders will be self-seeking, conceited, lifted with pride, having a form of godliness, but deny the power of sanctified living. These types of leaders are bound by lust and greed, having a love of pleasure more than a love of God.

These types of leaders are those who have their conscience seared as with a hot iron. Play acting the faith in hypocrisy, but this sort is creeping around seeking to beguile unstable souls by committing acts of immorality. While they continue to feast with you at the Lords table.

Leaders who have been shown the truth but have turned aside, every learning but not willing to live in the truth. Men who are opposed to the Holy Spirit, and some even walk-in demonic powers. They are resisting the truth, men of corruption, reprobate concerning the faith.
Ironically, Paul warns the Church of the last days will welcome evil men and imposters who are willing to itch their ears with Christian philosophy. These philosophies deny the doctrines of the faith and lead the Church into apostasy. Paul warns in the last days, Christians will not endure sound doctrines, but will instead heap to themselves corrupted teachers who will tell them the philosophical lies they want to hear.

2 Timothy 3:1-13 (81)
1 This know also, that in the last days perilous times shall come.
2 For men shall be lovers of their own selves, covetous, boasters, proud, blasphemers, disobedient to parents, unthankful, unholy,
3 Without natural affection, truce breakers, false accusers, incontinent, fierce, despisers of those that are good,
4 Traitors, heady, high minded, lovers of pleasures more than lovers of God.
5 Having a form of godliness but denying the power thereof: from such turn away.

6 For of this sort are they which creep into houses, and lead captive silly women laden with sins, led away with divers' lusts,
7 Ever learning, and never able to come to the knowledge of the truth.
8 Now as Jannes and Jambres withstood Moses, so do these also resist the truth: men of corrupt minds, reprobate concerning the faith.
9 But they shall proceed no further: for their folly shall be manifest unto all men, as theirs also was.
10 But thou hast fully known my doctrine, manner of life, purpose, faith, long suffering, charity, patience,
11 Persecutions, afflictions, which came unto me at Antioch, at Iconium, at Lystra; what persecutions I endured: but out of them all the Lord delivered me.
12 Yea, and all that will live godly in Christ Jesus shall suffer persecution.
13 But evil men and seducers shall wax worse and worse, deceiving, and being deceived.

Jesus Christ also warned Christians of end times deception including false Christs, false prophets, and lying signs and wonders. Also, the conditions of the world will be like the days of Noah before the great flood, and wide scale acceptance of sexual immorality like in the time of Lot and Sodom.

Matthew 24:37-39 (82)
37 But as the days of Noe were, so shall also the coming of the Son of man be.
38 For as in the days that were before the flood they were eating and drinking, marrying and giving in marriage, until the day that Noe entered the ark,
39 And knew not until the flood came, and took them all away; so, shall also the coming of the Son of man be.

What was Jesus Christ warning the Church to avoid? The last days will be filled with a spirit of lawlessness where men have abandoned all fear of God and are continuously breaking the laws of God. As the result of lawlessness abounding, the love of many Christians will grow cold as the pressures to compromise the faith are increased. It will seem God is doing nothing about the perversion which has grown upon the earth, and mankind seems to get away with sin and wickedness. The influences of a corrupted world, an immoral culture, will press Christians to compromise with the world.

Luke 21:34-36 (83)
34 And take heed to yourselves, lest at any time your hearts be overcharged with surfeiting, and drunkenness, and cares of this life, and so that day come upon you unawares.
35 For as a snare shall it come on all them that dwell on the face of the whole earth.

36 Watch ye therefore, and pray always, that ye may be accounted worthy to escape all these things that shall come to pass, and to stand before the Son of man.

What is Jesus Christ warning His disciples to watch and pray for? To escape the end times deception and trials which are coming upon the whole world, as a snare to capture every man into Satanic deception. When the cares of this life, the deceitfulness of riches, and the lusts of worldly things can enter the Christian who is not watching and choke his faith. In order to escape the end time deception which leads the Church into the Great Apostasy, the saints must watch and pray to be counted worthy to escape. Where is the escape, by rapture to stand before the Lord?

End time apostasy and deception is well documented in Scriptures by multiple original apostolic teachers who speak of end time peril. Let a man take heed to these warnings as the days which this book is being written are lawless times and the time of Tribulation is drawing near. Are we not seeing the great lawless spirit leading the world into denying Jesus Christ? Are there not evidences the Church is in a major departure from the authority of Scriptures, and Bible morality? Are not the last days which are perilous, now set before us? Take heed to yourselves lest any man think he stands untouched by these corrupting influences. Take heed, watch and pray lest you fall.

Chapter 13
Christians Victory Over Antichrist

Some Christians will obtain victory over the Antichrist by being raptured in a Pre-Tribulation rapture having never to face the Tribulation time at all. While others will be part of the Great Multitude which appear in rapture after a time of persecution enduring for a season, being overcome by the Antichrist. Some Christians will not escape either in the first or second rapture, instead will die as martyrs during this time. For those who die no rapture is possible, only the resurrection of the righteous as their names are written in the book of life. For rapture is about the living saints at the time of the Second Coming of the Lord, and the order of the Harvest at the end of the age.

The book of Revelation exhorts the Christians who are going through the time when Antichrist is waging war with the saints to be faithful. Christians must endure whatever lot will happen, in the face of martyrdom must keep the commandments of God, and not deny Jesus Christ committing apostasy. The Scriptures are clear those who die in the Lord during this time are considered martyrs for Christ and are blessed by keeping their testimony. Willing to die for the faith, then deny the faith in apostasy.

Revelation 14:12-13 (84)
12 Here is the patience of the saints: here are they that keep the commandments of God, and the faith of Jesus.
13 And I heard a voice from heaven saying unto me, Write, Blessed are the dead which die in the Lord from henceforth: Yea, saith the Spirit, that they may rest from their labors; and their works do follow them.

During the time of the Antichrist Gods judgments are being poured out in increasing severity. During this time, any person who turns to the Lord in genuine repentance can still be saved. However, listed during the Great Tribulation is a sin which can never be forgiven. A sin which Scriptures have listed as an unpardonable sin, identified as committed by those who receive the Mark of the Beast and worship the Antichrist. Anyone who takes the Mark of the Beast cannot be saved and is eternally punished in the Lake of Fire along with the Antichrist, and the False Prophet.

Revelation 19:19-20 (85)
19 And I saw the beast, and the kings of the earth, and their armies, gathered to make war against him that sat on the horse, and against his army.
20 And the beast was taken, and with him the false prophet that wrought miracles before him, with which he deceived them that had received the mark of the beast, and them that worshipped his image. These both were cast alive into a lake of fire burning with brimstone.

Martyrs of the Antichrist who got victory by not taking the Mark of the Beast have their victory suffering the death of martyrdom. They did not qualify for the first rapture, neither were they part of the Great Multitude in Heaven rapture which occurs during the time of the Great Tribulation. Instead died in defense of the faith during this time and are therefore qualified to rule with Jesus Christ during the coming Millennial Kingdom and are part of the first resurrection.

Revelation 20:4-6 (86)
4 And I saw thrones, and they sat upon them, and judgment was given unto them: and I saw the souls of them that were beheaded for the witness of Jesus, and for the word of God, and which had not worshipped the beast, neither his image, neither had received his mark upon their foreheads, or in their hands; and they lived and reigned with Christ a thousand years.
5 But the rest of the dead lived not again until the thousand years were finished. This is the first resurrection.
6 Blessed and holy is he that hath part in the first resurrection: on such the second death hath no power, but they shall be priests of God and of Christ and shall reign with him a thousand years.

The martyred saints of the Tribulation time are considered victorious in death and are rewarded as over-comers in Christ. Those souls who will be resurrected in the first resurrection, who were beheaded for the witness of Jesus, and for the Word of God. These saints though not being raptured endured the suffering which will manifest unto death during the Tribulation. They did not commit the unpardonable sin of taking the Mark of the Beast, and by death refusing to worship the Antichrist by which qualify for the Kingdom age. Neither had they received the Mark as a sign, a seal, in secret to avoid persecution while still maintaining their faith in Christ. For God will not allow any comprise of the faith in any act of denial where Christians deny their faith in apostasy to save their own lives. All such actions will be met with severity, as no apostate Christianity will led to deliverance during the Tribulation time. Only by rapture, by death, or in prison will Christians find their deliverance from the coming Tribulation. Watch and pray that you might be counted worthy to escape all these things which are about to come to try the whole world.

The Antichrist and Mark Will Fail

Christians must come to understand Gods way of deliverance is by complete trust and dependence upon Jesus Christ. Satan is always attempting to get Christians to compromise with the things of the world, in order to get them to bow their knees in compromise. Satan's tactics have always been the same since the temptation in the Garden, and even tried to get Jesus Christ to worship him in the wilderness temptation with those same tactics. Our basic needs to life must be given into the hands of God, and we must deny ourselves picking up the Cross in fellowshipping with the sufferings of Jesus Christ. For those Christians who compromise with the world, will not be approved at the Judgment Seat of Christ.

For those who are not raptured from the coming Tribulation the trails of the faith will be of the severest nature. Even though followers of the Antichrist seek protection from him rather than God, their devotion to Antichrist will all be in vain. As the judgments of God are the severest upon the Antichrist and his kingdom. In fact, the final bowls of Gods wrath are almost entirely directed at the Antichrist, his followers, and government.

Those who have thought to deny the Lord, take the Mark of the Beast will suffer immeasurable pain and torment. As great famines and plagues are set in judgment against the days of the Antichrist, food and water will become very scarce. Many of Gods judgments burn up the crops, and the make water undrinkable, also other types of famine and plagues.

No amount of humanity attempting to escape the judgments of God in those days will be met with relief. Instead, when the wrath of God is poured out upon all who took the Mark of the Beast comes a terrible plague of sores. With little food, or water, and complete physical discomfort from Gods plagues mankind while revile against heaven in blasphemy of God.

Revelation 16:1-11 (87)
1 And I heard a great voice out of the temple saying to the seven angels, go your ways, and pour out the vials of the wrath of God upon the earth.
2 And the first went and poured out his vial upon the earth; and there fell a noisome and grievous sore upon the men which had the mark of the beast, and upon them which worshipped his image.
3 And the second angel poured out his vial upon the sea; and it became as the blood of a dead man: and every living soul died in the sea.
4 And the third angel poured out his vial upon the rivers and fountains of waters; and they became blood.
5 And I heard the angel of the waters say, thou art righteous, O Lord, which art, and wast, and shalt be, because thou hast judged thus.
6 For they have shed the blood of saints and prophets, and thou hast given them blood to drink; for they are worthy.
7 And I heard another out of the altar say, even so, Lord God Almighty, true and righteous are thy judgments.
8 And the fourth angel poured out his vial upon the sun; and power was given unto him to scorch men with fire.
9 And men were scorched with great heat, and blasphemed the name of God, which hath power over these plagues: and they repented not to give him glory.

10 And the fifth angel poured out his vial upon the seat of the beast; and his kingdom was full of darkness; and they gnawed their tongues for pain,
11 And blasphemed the God of heaven because of their pains and their sores and repented not of their deeds.

The command given by God is for Christians to watch and pray. For those who have not obtained to the first rapture they must endure until the end.

Matthew 24:7-13 (88)
7 For nation shall rise against nation, and kingdom against kingdom: and there shall be famines, and pestilences, and earthquakes, in divers' places.
8 All these are the beginning of sorrows.
9 Then shall they deliver you up to be afflicted and shall kill you: and ye shall be hated of all nations for my name's sake.
10 And then shall many be offended, and shall betray one another, and shall hate one another. 11 And many false prophets shall rise and shall deceive many.
12 And because iniquity shall abound, the love of many shall wax cold.
13 But he that shall endure unto the end, the same shall be saved.

The first seals opened by Jesus Christ to usher in the Tribulation are all about war, famine, plagues, and pestilence. At the same time a spirit of lawlessness predominates the earth, in so much the world will come to hate the commandments of God and persecute the followers of Jesus Christ. In the face of Christian hatred, the saints will be tempted to deny their faith, so a Great Apostasy is predicted by Scriptures. During this time faith in Christ will bring about great suffering and persecution to such an extent that even natural bonds between family members will be tempted to dissolve. The members of one another's households will be offended and shall betray one another. A time is coming where a mother or father, might be delivered up by a son or daughter, or just the other way. All this will happen in the last days when Gods laws are being rejected and lawlessness abounds.

God Will Shorten the Days of Tribulation

The trial of the Christian faith is to be very severe in the last days. Jesus Christ warned of many dangers which would come to deceive if it were possible even the very elect. The exhortation for Christians is they must endure these trails to the very end. Of course, escape by rapture is promised to the faithful watching ones as a reward to their devotion to Jesus Christ. In teaching on the last days Jesus Christ warns those who are passing through these trails must endure to the very end in order to be saved.

Matthew 24:13 (89)
13 But he that shall endure unto the end, the same shall be saved.

God will commit to those who endure to the end in faithfulness to Him. Jesus Christ promises to liven them, and to grant them salvation and entrance into the Heavenly Kingdom at the Judgment. Jesus promised: "But he that shall endure unto the end, the same shall be saved" The Lord will cut short the days of the Great Tribulation. Why must this be done? Is it not because of the severity of judgments? If God were to continue to plague the world with all His wrath, who would then be able to survive in the end?

Due to the severity of the Great Tribulation, along with the persecution of Christians and the last seven plagues of Gods wrath, our Lord Jesus promised to shorten those days.

Matthew 24:22 (90)
"And except those days should be shortened, there should no flesh be saved: but for the elect's sake those days shall be shortened." (Matthew 24:22)

There is hope in the time of Great Tribulation, even though some Christians have missed the first rapture. The final years of Gods out pouring of wrath will be shortened to 3 ½ years. "Immediately after the distress of those days the sun will be darkened, and the moon will not give its light; the stars will fall from the sky, and the heavenly bodies will be shaken. Then will appear the sign of the Son of Man in heaven. And then the peoples

of the earth will mourn when they see the Son of Man coming on the clouds of heaven, with power and great glory. And He will send his angels with a loud trumpet call, and they will gather his elect from the four winds, from one end of the heavens to the other.'
(Matthew 24:29-31) (91)

We can see the teaching of Jesus Christ in Matthew chapter twenty-four matches with the prophetic judgments found in the Book of Revelation. Even the prophets of old spoke of these coming end time judgments and the wrath of God.

Isaiah 13:9-13 (92)
9 Behold, the day of the Lord cometh, cruel both with wrath and fierce anger, to lay the land desolate: and he shall destroy the sinners thereof out of it.
10 For the stars of heaven and the constellations thereof shall not give their light: the sun shall be darkened in his going forth, and the moon shall not cause her light to shine.
11 And I will punish the world for their evil, and the wicked for their iniquity; and I will cause the arrogancy of the proud to cease and will lay low the haughtiness of the terrible.
12 I will make a man more precious than fine gold, even a man than the golden wedge of Ophir. 13 Therefore I will shake the heavens, and the earth shall remove out of her place, in the wrath of the Lord of hosts, and in the day of his fierce anger.

Joel 3:12-15 (93)
12 Let the heathen be wakened and come up to the valley of Jehoshaphat: for there will I sit to judge all the heathen round about.
13 Put ye in the sickle, for the harvest is ripe: come, get you down; for the press is full, the fats overflow; for their wickedness is great.
14 Multitudes, multitudes in the valley of decision: for the day of the Lord is near in the valley of decision.
15 The sun and the moon shall be darkened, and the stars shall withdraw their shining.

The promise of escape by rapture has been made available to all Christians who remain faithful to watch and pray. To those Christians who sought out the warnings of Scriptures, the way to escape the coming Antichrist will be obvious. However, for those who are caught in the snare, whose mind is upon earthly matters, and who love this present world the warnings of Christ will have fallen upon deaf ears. Jesus Christ spoke and warned of these things so the saints could be girded, and their lamps lit, watching for when their master would arrive to remove them from harm's way.

All Christians who are following the Lord will suffer persecution in this present evil age. For those who are alive during the time of the Tribulation escape is possible, so the faithful watching prayerful saints will escape to safety when the Lord opens the door to heaven in the first rapture. Now is the time to watch and prayer looking for the blessed hope of the Lords appearing.

Chapter 14
Objections to Multiple Raptures

The questions concerning the first fruits Pretribulation rapture, and other raptures must be addressed by Scriptures. We must consider the fact many Christians see all the Church taken at the start of the Tribulation, no matter their spiritual condition. Which invalidates the warnings to watch and pray so we can escape the trials of the Tribulation. Multiple passages show escape is possible, while multiple passages also demonstrate being left through a portion of the Tribulation is also possible. This would be a possible explanation as to why some Christian teachers use passages for Pre-Tribulation, others Mid or Post Tribulation Scriptures. Does this in fact confirm multiple raptures based upon the readiness of Harvest; first fruits, general harvest, and gleanings? So, let us address some objections to multiple rapture doctrine.

All Christians are taken in rapture at the same time:

   I) Some Christians are raptured before the Throne, while others are taken into the air. Revelation 12:5 demonstrates the man child is taken from earth up to the Throne of God, who was to rule the nations with the rod of iron. This is a direct reference to the over comers at the Church of Philadelphia promised escape by Jesus Christ. Who also are promised the right to rule the nations with a rod of iron? So, Jesus Christ taught some Christians would escape who were Philadelphia, who kept the word of His patience: (Revelation 3:10). "Because you have kept the word of My patience, I will keep you from the hour of temptation, which shall come upon all the world, to try them that dwell upon the earth." Escape from the Tribulation is possible, while other are suffering loss during the Tribulation.

In addition to these verses, Revelation 12:5 speaks of being caught up to the throne of God. Revelation 14:3 says that these ones are before the throne. Luke 21:36 says that they will be placed before the Son of Man. All these refer to a rapture to heaven. But there are also other verses that speak of being raptured to the air. For example, 1 Thessalonians 4:17 says "to meet the Lord in the air," and Matthew 25:10 says, the bridegroom came; and those who were ready went in with him to the wedding feast. This also happens in the air. The harvest in Revelation 14:14-16 also takes place in the air. If the rapture all takes place before the tribulation, or all after the tribulation, how can these two groups of verses be explained? Therefore, it is indeed a biblical teaching to say that a minority of the believers will be raptured before the tribulation, whereas most of them will be raptured during the tribulation. Otherwise, it would be impossible to explain many verses.

Revelation chapter 14 is well into the Tribulation before the harvest is reaped by the Lord sitting upon the cloud in the mid heaven (sky). This matches with 1 Thessalonians 4:17 teach the saints meet the Lord in the air. This gathering is not like the first fruits which is taken all the way into the Throne room. Instead, this harvest ascends into the clouds gathering in the sky, which likely represents the Great Multitude which comes out of the Great Tribulation. (Revelation 7:14)

Argument of Two Comings

> II) No one knows the day of the Coming of Jesus Christ while at the same time the Christ's coming can be known by the signs. On the one hand Christ comes at the sounding of the seventh Trumpet, or the blowing of the last Trumpet. While on the other hand the Bible teaches Christ comes when you do not expect it, that day and hour which no man knows. Why such a diversity, unless the first rapture is not known, the thief like coming. The next rapture(s) are much more known by the signs (last trumpet).

Separation of the Body of Christ

III) Many say the rapture of the Church cannot be at several separate times as it violates the principle of the body of Christ. If there be more than one rapture the body of Christ would be separated from one another.

However, there are many passages of Scriptures which show distinctions among the different members of the body of Christ. Many of these distinctions are recognized at the Second Coming like the parables of the Talents, Pounds, and Ten Virgins. None of these distinctions violate the principle of the body of Christ, only differences in companies of peoples who have qualified for rewards or their loss. So, the same principle of multiple raptures where some Christians are rewarded when continuing in prayerful and watchful faithfulness before the coming of the Lord. While others miss the opportunity by their being caught up with the cares and riches of this world. Some saints are taken while others are left behind, not a violation of the body of Christ.

Rapture is free grace, not by any works.

IV) Some argue the redemption of the body is based upon grace therefore cannot be based upon fulfilling any conditions. If rapture is by grace, then some should not be taken while others left behind. However, whenever we find conditions being placed upon Christians, usually indicated by the word "if," then those conditions must be meet by fulling those conditions. So even though everything in the Christian faith requires the grace of God, grace does not invalidate personal responsibility. Even though the redemption of the body is guaranteed by grace the gift of salvation, the order of the Resurrection is based upon conditions. The apostle Paul clearly taught he was seeking the first resurrection as a prize and high calling to which he had not yet attained. Paul understood he must bring his body under subjection lest after preaching to other he would be disqualified. Obviously, Paul was teaching conditions on the order of the resurrection. Raptures are just a part of meeting those conditions, being taken or left behind. In the end all Christians will be resurrected, however some will be raptured and resurrected before others.

Multiple raptures defeat the hope of the Second Coming.

V)   Some who protest the multiple rapture position, protest it defeats the hope of His coming. Teaching only a small minority will be raptured before others (first fruits), while the majority (Great Multitude) will pass through some portion of the Tribulation.

The blessed hope of His appearing is also based upon Godly living, all saints who are purifying themselves, as the Bride has made herself ready. Even though all saints while have the hope of resurrection, not all will be qualified as the Bride of Christ (Parable of Ten Virgins). The first fruits harvest includes the chaste virgins of Christ who follow Jesus Christ wherever He goes. Does the whole Church qualify for the Bride, even though the resurrection is promised to all? Knowing some will not qualify as the five wise virgins, does not in any way reduce the blessed hope of His coming. Only loss of Bridal qualification for those who in this present age do not make themselves ready for His coming.

Hard to prove rapture and resurrection are connected.

VI) Some protest the 1 Corinthians 15:23 passage does not indicate any conditions as how to qualify for the first rapture, only, Christ, the first fruits, then those who are Christ's at His coming. Which in fact is true, as these passage only demonstrate an order to the resurrection, not an order to the rapture.

Here are two facts about this passage 1) An order to the Resurrection 2) Does not disprove multiple raptures. It only addressed the fact of resurrection while other passages demonstrate how this is brought about. To teach there are not multiple raptures because they are not mentioned here, is to take a single passage and build an incomplete theology around it. In confirmation of the living being changed at the trump of God confirms that being caught up and transformed into immortality demonstrates rapture and resurrection are connected. So, we must take all the Scriptures into consideration.

(1 Corinthians 15:51-53) "Behold I will show you a mystery; we shall not all sleep, but we all shall be changed. In a moment, in the twinkling of an eye, at the last Trump; for the

Trumpet shall sound, and the dead shall be raised incorruptible, and we shall be changed. For this corruptible must put on incorruption, and this mortal must put on immortality."

In this passage Christians are taken at the Trump of God and transformed into immortality. Those who are alive are taken and transformed in a moments time, from mortality into immortality. The process happens at the Second Coming, the saints rise to meet with the Lord, an arrangement at the Judgment Seat, then qualified glorified immortal saints descend with the Lord to rule with Christ on earth.

There is only one rapture.

VII) Now some Christians will protest does not 1 Corinthians 15:51, teach only one rapture? "We all will be changed," teaches everyone will be transformed at the same time? It is true all Christians will all be changed by resurrection, but it does not say we all will be raptured at the same time. So, reading this into the passage, teaching one rapture, only at the time of the Second Coming, does not address passages which speak to an order to the rapture. This passage is about the resurrection, it is promises of transformation into immortality. It does not say, there is only one rapture, just because all saints will in the end be made immortal.

Christians should not fear Gods judgments.

VIII) Some Christians protest it is wrong to be afraid of God and judgment. Many imagine that believers should only respect or reverence God. They therefore are opposed to the idea of truly fearing Him: Isaiah 8: 13 Sanctify the LORD of hosts himself; and let him be your FEAR and let him be your DREAD. But notice that the Bible uses "fear" alongside reverence: Hebrews 12: 28 Wherefore we receiving a kingdom which cannot be moved, let us have grace, whereby we may serve God acceptably with reverence and godly fear: 29 For our God is a consuming fire. Verse 29 would make no sense unless "godly fear" means real fear. The concept of multiple raptures flies in the face all Christians will receive the same rewards no matter their walk of consecration. However, the gift of grace is not judged, instead works of reward based upon meeting certain conditions. Then Christians must face the Scriptures which speak of judgment, loss and even punishment at the Second Coming of Jesus Christ.

There is no condemnation for believers.

IX) What about the promise's believers will not be condemned? The first text often cited to object to accountability truth is Romans 8:1. Does not Romans 8:1 teach that there is no condemnation for Christians? Romans 8:1 "There is therefore now no condemnation to them which are in Christ Jesus, who walk not after the flesh, but after the Spirit." The idea Christians are measured in the fires of Gods judgment are repulsive to many Christians believing it condemns the saved. What is judged or condemned are the "works of the flesh," while the believers salvation remains intact.

Works related raptures are legalism.

X) Is not works related raptures legalism? True legalism is turning our eyes to works for justification in eternity. It has to do with working for initial salvation, which is given through faith alone. However, there are many passages of Scriptures which teach promises based upon Christians meeting certain conditions. Hebrews 6: 11, "And we desire that every one of you do shew the same diligence to the full assurance of hope unto the end: 12 That ye be not slothful, but followers of them who through faith and patience inherit the promises." In this case the believer is required to meet conditions after coming into saving faith. Multiple raptures have "conditional promises," which do not invalidate salvation by grace alone, instead are works for future reward, or their loss.

Warnings in Scriptures are only for the Jews.

XI) Do the warnings of Scriptures apply solely to Jews or Tribulation Saints? When Christians are confronted with Biblical accountability based upon conditions they often reply, these warnings do not apply to Christians. Like when the warnings of judgment are given in the Book of Hebrews, they suppose them to be for the Jewish Christians of those days only. Also, when Jesus Christ warns of judgment or loss, they say its only for the Jews during the time of Jesus Christ. Also, warnings of the Book of Revelation demonstrating how Christians suffer loss, are for Tribulation saints only as the Church has already been raptured.

The Cross of Jesus Christ has given Christians rapture.

XII) Did not Jesus Christ pay for our sins at Calvary? Jesus paid for all our sins, past, present and future, as far as eternal salvation is concerned. The distinction in Scripture is therefore between temporary and eternal judgment. Christians can never be judged eternally for their sins since Jesus has paid the full price for them on the Cross. Yet, the sins of believers can bring temporal judgments, as demonstrated by parables of the Pounds, Talents, and 10 Virgins. The forgiveness of sins regarding believers is not automatic, and it must be maintained (Matthew 6: 15, 18: 35, 1 John 1: 9). For those who refuse those warnings the consequences will be seen at the Judgment Seat of Christ, and even for some in the order of their rapture position.

Most Christians are Pre-Tribulation rapture

XIII) Shouldn't We Follow the Majority? Christians must follow the Word of God, not the popular, religious majority. In fact, it has been proven repeatedly that the majority (especially in an age of religious corruption) is usually wrong. The Bible speaks about the religious majority in the last days, and it is not a Godly Christ centered Church. "I charge thee therefore before God, and the Lord Jesus Christ, who shall judge the quick and the dead at his appearing and his kingdom; 2 Preach the word; be instant in season, out of season; reprove, rebuke, exhort with all long suffering and doctrine. 3 For the time will come when they will not endure sound doctrine; but after their own lusts shall they heap to themselves teachers, having itching ears; 4 And they shall turn away their ears from the truth, and shall be turned unto fables." (2 Timothy 4:1-4)

Conclusion
Why End Time Rapture Wars

In this book I have written about the doctrine of Premillennialism and the coming Tribulation. In this context I have endeavored to explain the significance of the catching up of the saints at the coming of the Lord. I have used Church history, the testimony of Church fathers, and most importantly the testimony of Scriptures to confirm the reality of what is called the rapture by the modern Church. Now I want to finalize the reasons why the modern Church is moving away from a coming Tribulation, the appearing of the Antichrist, and the removal of living saints by rapture.

    1) Rejection of Historic Premillennialism
In writing on the position of early Church fathers it is undeniable by any true Church historian, the

position of the first century Church was premillennial. Early Christians in the face of martyrdom encouraged one another not to deny their faith. The belief in a coming Kingdom age was to be their reward by faithfully suffering in keeping the testimony of the faith.

Christians must consider the "kingdom future position," held by first century Christians. For two hundred years Jewish Christians defended the coming Kingdom willing to suffer martyrdom instead of compromising the faith. The premillennial position was held until the time of Constantine and the paganization of organized Church. At that time Constantine declared the Church was declared to be the Kingdom of Heaven on earth. The new position was declared to be "a Millennial," with no future Kingdom. This was the beginning of the corruption of the true eschatological position, held by Historic Premillennialism.

2) Rejection of Church Fathers About Coming Tribulation

Even after the first two centuries notable Church fathers continued to speak of a coming Son of Perdition, the Antichrist. This proves none of the early Church fathers thought Matthew chapter 24 was fulfilled at the destruction of the Temple in 70 AD by General Titus of Rome. Instead, Church Fathers continued to warn of coming false Messiah, and worldwide deception. Included in this warning was a Tribulation time when the Antichrist would deceive the whole known world. Even though Rome and Cesar Nero were considered a persecutor of the Jews, Nero was not thought to be the Antichrist of Revelation, Matthew, or Daniel.

3) The Allegorizing of Scriptures
So now the modern Church wants to put the Antichrist and Tribulation in history. In order to accomplish this the historical position of the Church must be denied, as well as the witness of the Church fathers. However, the most damning record against a historical Antichrist is the record of scriptures themselves. In order to make the Scriptures say something they have never intended you must twist the doctrines. This has become common practice in modern Church teaching especially in eschatological practices like the Book of Revelation. The twisted of Scriptures is legitimized by an allegorical practice of removing the literal interpretation of the Word of God, and making it a symbol, type or allegory. Then the teacher can adapt their own meaning or philosophy injecting into the Word typologies which fit with their end time scenarios. Of course, all this is rejected of Christians hold to the literal historical grammatical way of interpreting the written Word of God. Simply put the best way to read and interpret the Scriptures is in a straightforward plain literal meaning.

4) Dominion Theology
Now with the injecting of man-made philosophy the driving force is a worldwide Church take over. This was the same way of thinking in early Catholicism where the Church attempted to control the nations of the world. Let us look at the belief the Church will Christianize the world before the Second Coming of Jesus Christ. No future coming Antichrist, no coming Tribulation, no catastrophic ending to this age, instead a worldwide Church take over. So where would Christians need to watch and pray for an end time deception. In short, this philosophy has no need or place for a catching away of the saints to remove them from danger. Rapture or removal of the Church is viewed as escapism by Dominion Theology /Kingdom Now teachers.

5) Preterism
With the increase of Dominion Theology, Preterism has arisen to give an allegorical twisting of the Book of Revelation. Preterism must deny the rapture as in their philosophy the prophetic judgments of Revelation were fulfilled in 70 AD. As no saints were raptured in 70 AD, Preterists want to eliminate any Scriptures which teach a future removal of the Church, or a coming future Antichrist. The growing acceptance of Preterist Theology also points to the decrease in the Scriptures as final authority in the modern Church. Many saints who teach the Word of God no longer believe in its infallibility.

6) Elimination of All Judgment
With manmade philosophy replacing the authority of Scriptures, many modern Christian teachers say all judgment of God has passed. This rise in the elimination of all future judgment is seen in doctrines like; Dominion Theology, Preterism, Universal Salvation and Hyper Grace. What remains for many in these camps is only a golden age of humanity and worldwide Church takeover of the world. Obviously, a golden age of humanity has man saving the world, no need to escape by rapture, or a failed Church and apostasy. The question is who controls the nations at the end of the age? A Church which has fallen into a Great Apostasy will be soundly defeated by Antichrist deception. Only the faithful will escape into heaven by rapture, avoiding the catastrophic judgments which end this age. The Church has come to a strong line of division between the pre-Millennial position, and Kingdom Now, Millennial Now. No Christian can hold both positions as they are diametrically opposed to one another.

7) Rise in False Prophets
With the acceptance of man-made doctrines and philosophy by the modern Church, is the necessity of those who will teach false doctrines. Jesus Christ warned of false prophets in the last days. Also, the apostle Paul warned of the departure of Christians

into apostasy, steaming from seductive teachers and doctrines of demons. The Church in the last days is being flooded by false teachers, false apostles and prophets. In the last days, many saints will not want to hear sound doctrine anymore. Instead, will heap to themselves teachers who will itch their ears with worldly lusts. A Church which has fallen into end time deception, will not need to watch a pray to escape by rapture the things which are coming upon the whole world as a snare. Also, will be seduced into apostasy by false prophets and doctrine of demons.

8} A Denial of Bodily Resurrection
The spiritualizing of the first resurrection written in Revelation chapter twenty. Instead of admitting all those events are a description of events which transpire at the defeat of the Antichrist, and the chaining of Antichrist into the abyss. The kingdom now teachers wants to spiritualize those events placing them at the first coming of Jesus Christ, instead of the Second Coming. They insist this passage is just allegorical, making the first resurrection a spiritual one without a need for a bodily resurrection. This places Christians already in glory with Jesus Christ in heaven. No need for a rapture into glory, as the glory has already been given when Jesus Christ raised from the dead. A direct attack on the authority of the Written Word

of God, and excuse to deny the first resurrection as "literal in body."

8) A Golden Age of Humanity
Many religions are looking for an age of Aquarius a golden age of man, led by a Christ like person. When the Church agrees with a coming age of Aquarius before the Second Coming of Jesus Christ, the Church plays into the coming one world government of Antichrist. It will be no surprise when the Harlot Church in Revelation chapters 17 and 18 aligns itself with the Antichrist government. A golden age Church is seeking unity in an Ecumenical Movement and Interfaith Movement for a super end time world take over Church. There is no need for a Church rapture in a golden age, for why should Christians escape when there is no danger.

10) Spirit of Antichrist in Church
Finally, with all these factors and others working in place the spirit of antichrist is gaining ascendency in the last days Church. All these factors are the footprint of the coming Son of Perdition, the literal Antichrist. The Church seems to have fallen into antichrist deception, often denying the doctrines of Scriptures which would expose its presence. No sense of imminent coming of the Lord. Neither a watching in prayer to avoid the coming deep darkness which will fill the nations of the earth. The belief in a coming worldwide deception by a

coming false Messiah is falling away from mainstream Christians.

As false doctrines take precedence, the need for Christians to escape from end time catastrophic judgments is being considered old fashioned, outdated beliefs. The doctrine of rapture, the catching up of the saints is at war with modern Christian Theology. A major shift in eschatology is happening right in our day. Rapture wars represents the battle among Christians who are debating what end time scenario is authentic Bible truth. The doctrine of rapture has come to a doctrinal forefront as a battle with the spirit of antichrist. I pray modern Christians will not lightly dismiss Gods way of escape in the last days.

Final Thoughts
Over Coming Fear of the End Days

As the last years of this age are determined to be the Tribulation, with the coming Antichrist, and Gods prophetic judgments. What is the best way to maintain the faith, and not be overcome with fear? The best way to overcome a fear of the end of days is to be make ready for the Second Coming of the Lord. The Lord commands His disciples to watch and pray so the trials which are to come as a snare upon the whole world will not overtake you. Be dressed and ready with your lamps bringing bright. So, when the Lord opens the door to the first rapture nothing holds you to this present evil age from your escape.

The Scriptures warn the saints as to what will happen at the end of the age and escape is possible. The Bible affirms saints who are prepared will be taken in rapture away from the coming Tribulation, and before the Throne of God. Only those who are not awake in watchful prayer will be left behind to face the coming Antichrist. So instead of fear, have faith in God. Though these things be impossible for mere men to accomplish nothing is impossible with God. Surely the Lord can provide the way of escape for those are qualified for the first rapture. Our encouragement is to view the Second Coming with expectation and hope:
"But we do not want you to be uninformed, brothers, about those who are asleep, that you may not grieve as others do who have no hope. For since we believe that Jesus died and rose again, even so, through Jesus, God will bring with him those who have fallen asleep. For this we declare to you by a word from the Lord, that we who are alive, who are left until the coming of the Lord, will not precede those who have fallen asleep. For the Lord himself will descend from heaven with a cry of command, with the voice of an archangel, and with the sound of the trumpet of God. And the dead in Christ will rise first. Then we who are alive, who are left, will be caught up together with them in the clouds to meet the Lord in the air, and so we will always be with the Lord. Therefore encourage one another with these words."

(1 Thessalonians 4:13-18) (94)

This book is written to encourage the brethren in Christ to prepare for the coming of the Lord. For the Spirit and the Bride say, "Come Lord Jesus."

Bibliography for Rapture Wars
Chapter One

1. (1 Thessalonians 4:13-18) KJV
2. (2 Peter 3:3-4) KJV
3. (2 Peter 3:17) KJV
4. (Hebrews 11:6-7) KJV
5. (1 Corinthians 15:51) KJV
6. (1 Corinthians 15:35-58) KJV

Chapter Two

7. (1 Thessalonians 4:13-18) KJV

Chapter Three

8. Kingdom Now theology is influenced by the Latter Rain movement,[27] and critics have connected it to the New Apostolic Reformation,[28] "Spiritual Warfare Christianity,"[27] and Fivefold ministry thinking.[29]" (Wikipedia)

9. https://www.gotquestions.org/seven-mountain-mandate.html

10. Historically, preterists and non-preterists have generally agreed that the Jesuit Luis de Alcasar (1554–1613) wrote the first systematic preterist exposition of prophecy - Vestigatio arcani sensus in Apocalypsi (published in 1614)—during the Counter-Reformation." (Wikipedia)

Chapter Four

11. Pre-tribulation rapture theology was popularized extensively in the 1830s by John Nelson Darby and the Plymouth Brethren,[1] and further popularized in the United States in the early 20th century by the wide circulation of the Scofield Reference Bible." (Wikipedia)

12. The vast majority of dispensationalists profess the Pretribulation rapture, with small minorities professing to either a mid-tribulation or post-tribulation rapture." (Wikipedia)

13. (Philip Schaff, History of the Christian Church, 2:614)

14. 1. Johannes Quasten, Patrology, Vol. 1 (Westminster, Maryland: Christian Classics, Inc.), 219.
15. "Dialogue with Trypho (Chapters 31-47)". Newadvent.org. Retrieved 2014-01-24.

16. (Didache - Chapter 16)

17. (First Apology of Justin, Chapter 110)

18. (Against Heresies V, XXVI, 1)

19. (On the Resurrection of the Flesh, Chapter 25)

20. Treatise on Christ and Antichrist, 61

21. Epistle of Cyprian LV, 1,2

22. Epistles of Cyprian, LIII, p.722

23. Commentary on the Apocalypse, 20:1-3

24. In Against Heresies 5:29 Irenaeus

25. Treatise of Cryptian

26. treatise called; The Last Times.

27. https://www.logosapostolic.org/bible_study/RP355-9ChurchFathers.htm

28. Wikipedia

29. Curt Aland: History of Christianity: From the Beginnings to the Threshold of the Reformation, vol 1 Philadelphia Fortress Press; 1, 87

30. Aland, History of Christianity, I, 92.

Chapter 5

31. Wikipedia

32. Wikipedia

33. Don Pirozok: Kingdom Come; A Biblical Response to Dominion Theology, Pilgrims Progress Publishing pgs. 52-53

34. Revelation 20:1-6 KJV

35. Wikipedia

36. Wikipedia

Chapter Six

37. Matthew 24:1-3 KJV

38. MichaelBaxter:
http://www.themillennialkingdom.org.uk/ParousiaAndEpiphany.htm

Chapter Seven

39. 1 Thessalonians 5:2-3 KJV

40. Matthew 24:40-41 KJV

41. Matthew 24:42-44 KJV

42. Matthew 24:45-47 KJV

43. Matthew 24:48-51 KJV

44. Watchman Nee:"The King and the Kingdom", p. 271 CFP, Co. 1978)

Chapter Eight

45. 1 Corinthians 15:22-27 KJV

46. Revelation 5:9-14 KJV

47. Revelation 14:1-5 KJV

48. Hebrews 11:5 KJV

49. Revelation 7:9-17 KJV

50. Revelation 13:7-10 KJV

Chapter Nine

51. 1 Corinthians 15:51-53 KJV

52. 1 Thessalonians 4:13-18 KJV

53. 2 Thessalonians 2:1-3 KJV

54. 1 Thessalonians 4:16 KJV

55. Revelation 10:7 KJV

56. 1 Thessalonians 4:13-17 KJV

57. Collected Works of Watchman Nee, the (Set 1) Vol. 15: Study on Matthew, chapter 14 section 6.

58. Collected Works of Watchman Nee, the (Set 1) Vol. 19: Notes on Scriptural Messages (3), Chapter 9, Section 5)

Chapter Ten

59. GH Lange First Fruits and Harvest Chapter 4 Pre-Tribulation Rapture

60. In the Appendix to his small work on The Song of Songs, entitled Union and Communion (ed. 5, p. 83),

61. Robert Chapman about the year 1896 issued a series of Suggestive Questions. Number 10 includes the following:

62. Robert Govett; The Parousia of Christ; The Hinders.

63. JA Seiss; The Apocalypse Seventh Lecture

64. J A Seiss; The Apocalypse: Seventh Lecture

65. The Theocratic Kingdom GNH Peters: Proposition 130: The Kingdom Is Preceded by the Translation of the Living Saints

66. THE COMING TRANSLATION OF WATCHFUL CHRISTIANSG. H. Pember, M.A.

67. [* The following is taken from
Mr. Panton's Evangelical Magazine - (THE
DAWN, vol. 13., No. 9, December 15th. 1936.) (1)

68. Philip Schaff in Lange's Commentary on Matthew

69. Joseph Augustus Seiss, The Parable of The Ten Virgins (1862).

70. George N.H. Peters, The Theocratic Kingdom, vol. 3 (Grand Rapids: Kregel), 306.

71. (Excerpt from: The Rod Will God Spare It: Kindle Position Chapter 26 Accountability Truth in History pt. 1)

72. Oswald J. Smith, Is the Antichrist at Hand? (Tabernacle Publishers, 1927)
Chapter Eleven
73. 2 Thessalonians 2:6-9 KJV

74. Revelation 12:5-9 KJV

75. Revelation 12:10-12 KJV

76. Revelation 13:5-10 KJV

77. 2 Thessalonians 2:3-4 KJV

78. Revelation 9:13-21 KJV

Chapter Twelve

79. 2 Thessalonians 2:1-3 KJV

80. 1 Timothy 4:1-2 KJV

81. 2 Timothy 3:1-13 KJV

82. Matthew 24:37-39 KJV

83. Luke 21:34-36 KJV

Chapter Thirteen

84. Revelation 14:12-13 KJV

85. Revelation 19:19-20 KJV

86. Revelation 20:4-6 KJV

87. Revelation 16:1-11 KJV

88. Matthew 24:7-13 KJV

89. Matthew 24:13 KJV

90. Matthew 24:22 KJV

91. Matthew 24:29-31 KJV

92. Isaiah 13:9-13 KJV

93. Joel 3:12-15 KJV

Chapter Fourteen

Conclusion
94. 1 Thessalonians 4:13-18 KJV

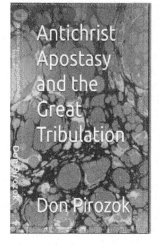

Made in the USA
Monee, IL
25 November 2020